From th   to Ireland

A Voyage of Discovery

VISING BENAVIDEZ-KENNEDY

Book and cover designer: Joy Watford

Editorial coordinator: Vanda Marie Brady

DEDICATION

To my husband Jim, and children Patrick and Noriana, who, tested by time, have shown their mettle in the ways of integration and biculturalism.

To the second generation of Filipinos in Ireland, I wish you peace and harmony, joy and great expectations as you plant your roots here. You will feel Irish and will live like the Irish, but deep down you will remain Filipino. You might stray for a while but in time you will seek to find your heritage and reach out for your homeland. I wish you an exciting voyage of self-discovery.

CONTENTS

ACKNOWLEDGEMENTS

Utang na loob is an important social currency in the Philippines and my debt of gratitude for all the information and insights put in this book is endless. Many published sources were sought and dissected, online researches browsed, consulted and collated.

For the direct assistance, a big thank you to Vanda Marie Brady, the talented and big-hearted Chairman of ENFiD (European Network of Filipino Diaspora) Ireland, whose inspiration and encouragement made me finish this book. To Joy Watford, my editor from the UK, whose professionalism lit the way to self-publishing. To Michael Ancheta, founder of the Filipino Forum and media specialist, who is always there when his expertise is needed. Last, but not least, to the Philippine Honorary Consul Mark Congdon for his invaluable support and assistance to this project.

Maraming salamat po.

FOREWORD

From the Philippines to Ireland: A Voyage of Discovery offers an overview of the life of Vising Kennedy and her fellow Filipino migrants as they came to Ireland. Vising portrays an honest and eye-opening account of her journey through reflections and research, shining a light on what many migrant workers currently experience in the Republic of Ireland.

This book comes at an opportune time as we work in the Philippine Honorary Consulate to strive to provide meaningful support on migration issues which both concern and interest the Filipino nationals in the Republic of Ireland. This serves as a useful tool in helping Filipino migrants deal with cultural integration issues and challenges. It shows the effects of cultural assimilation while equally cherishing the core roots of your birth place and the unavoidable course of emotions you can expect to go through to strive for that balance of identity.

It also enlightens us on the wonderful similarities between Filipino and Irish cultures and particularly love of family. It offers compassion, and gives hope and a sense of belonging to migrants who may be in challenging situations.

If you are considering migrating to a foreign country, then this book will help to guide you on the unexpected pitfalls and wonders of such an exciting adventure. It is unique and surely a work to treasure. So read it, enjoy it and learn from it. Thank you, Vising, for your wonderful insight and depth of clarity in producing this exceptional book.

Sincerely,

Mark Christopher Congdon
Honorary Consul of the Philippines
in Ireland

When dedicated community leader Michael Ancheta mentioned to me a book in the making about a Filipina's historical account on her personal journey in Ireland, I knew it was an opportunity that couldn't be missed.

I am glad to be of help in publishing this in-depth piece of work on the history of the Philippine-Ireland connection over several decades. It brings a new light to the harsh challenges of integration among Filipino migrants in Ireland as it promotes the belief that 'cultural differences are not threats to be overcome but a challenge to be enjoyed.'

As Vising makes her own way wandering the Emerald Isle, she suggests refreshing alternatives to tame culture shock by knowing what makes the Filipino Filipino, and the Irish Irish, while at the same time highlighting similarities between Filipino and Irish cultures.

From the Philippines to Ireland: A Voyage of Discovery chronicles an inspiring journey of inner reflection, self-maturation and discovery, and reveals what many migrant workers currently experience. I encourage everyone to read this book because its remarkable wisdom goes beyond the unique peculiarities of a migrant and beyond the borders of Ireland. It will move anyone trying to find themselves and their true identity in any part of the world.

Vanda Marie Brady

European Network of Filipino Diaspora–Ireland (ENFiD–Ireland)

ENFiD–Ireland is an open and collaborative undertaking to promote effective interconnectedness in the Euro-Filipino migrant community in order to affect relevant developments in Europe and the Philippines. It also believes in honing the ambassadorial potential of Euro-Pinoys by engaging them to their Philippine roots and the Irish cultural heritage, giving form to their identity as Filipino and Irish and promoting the Philippines & the Republic of Ireland. The Philippine Honorary Consulate in Dublin strives to provide timely and efficient frontline consular services to approximately 13,000 Filipino nationals in the Republic of Ireland.

PREFACE

Dear Filipinos in Ireland, would you believe that our ties with our Irish friends go all the way back to the 19th century?

Our story begins with that of a young Irish woman named Josephine and our national hero, Jose Rizal.

A Love Story

The year was 1895. Josephine Bracken arrived in a secluded area in the southern part of the Philippines to become the first Irish person to establish a connection of lasting value with our country.

Josephine Bracken was born in Victoria Barracks in Hong Kong on 9 August 1876 to an Irish couple, Cpl James Bracken and Elizabeth McBride. Her mother died after giving birth to her and because her father, a military man, was always on the move, Josephine was adopted by an American couple, Mr and Mrs George Edward Taufer. Mr Taufer worked as an engineer in Hong Kong and was widowed when Josephine was a child. In his old age, Mr. Taufer fell ill from a double cataract that no ophthalmologist in Hong Kong could cure. The search for a medical remedy took Josephine and her foster father to as far as Dapitan in Zamboanga, Philippines, where Dr Jose Rizal was exiled by the Spanish colonial government. It was love at first sight for Jose. Shortly after they met, he articulated his feelings in this poem:

> Josephine, Josephine
> Who to these shores have come
> Looking for a nest, a home,
> Like a wandering swallow;
> If your fate is taking you
> To Japan, China or Shanghai,
> Don't forget that on these shores
> A heart for you beats high.

Sadly, Jose couldn't save the old man from his incurable illness, but his love for Josephine was immovable, despite their short and tragic relationship. Josephine was immortalised in his famous last poem *'Mi Ultimo Adios'* ('My Last Farewell') as his 'sweet foreigner, my friend, my delight.' In honour of Rizal's *dulce estranjera*, the city government of Manila named one of its streets Josefina, (the Spanish equivalent of Josephine). Josefina Street crosses España Street near the Quezon City boundary.

Migration experts may not consider this romantic event as significant enough to establish social and historic ties between Ireland and the Philippines, but to many Filipinos, nothing embodied our countries' connection better than Josephine and Jose's relationship.

Isagani R. Medina, a distinguished Filipino historian, wrote in *Heritage* magazine in 1997:

> 'Josephine Bracken remains a shining star in Philippine history. Not only because she meant happiness to our hero, but also she was his clinical assistant, a 'nurse' so to speak, and later after his death, she joined the revolutionary Philippine army and served as a nurse on the battlefields. . .. I have featured Josephine as a forerunner of nurses and dental assistants in the Philippines.'

Josephine's great-grandson and biographer Macario Ofilada pays tribute to her short but intense life in his book *Errante Golondrina*:

> 'She has already entered into Philippine history as a major figure. Her association with Rizal in itself, their mutual love and what came out of this mutual love: the collaboration, the support, the encouragement, the battles, and even a stillborn son, placed Josephine in the map of Philippine historiography. Perhaps we can consider her as one of the unsung heroes of Philippine history.'

The Missionary Brigade

The beginning of the 20th century brought us the incredible story of Irish missionaries who left Ireland to bring their skills, energy and entrepreneurial flair to the less fortunate throughout the world. In 1929, hundreds of them were deployed to the Philippines to fill in the pastoral void left by the departure of Spanish friars from the country during the American colonial era. Thousands of Filipinos were educated and spiritually nourished by the Irish. In the province of Zambales where I lived, the Columban Fathers built a school in every parish. The Redemptorists in Metro Manila built the famous shrine of Our Lady of Perpetual Help in Baclaran where thousands of devotees seek solace in the weekly novena. The De La Salle Brothers set up schools in several towns and cities for poor and rich students alike. Out in the remote islands of Mindanao and the Visayas, the Presentation Sisters, the Columbans, the Divine Word Congregation, the Augustinians and the Good Shepherd Sisters and several others set up schools, pastoral centres, retreat houses and churches, all catering to large numbers of Filipino Catholics.

The Diplomatic Connection

For two centuries, immigration flowed in one direction between Ireland and the Philippines. That is, until the 1970s when a trickle of Filipinas started arriving in Ireland. Armed with their marriage certificates, they visited the office of the Department of Justice in Dublin and in one week, they got their Irish citizenship! I am one of these ladies—I met and married an Irishman in 1977 and came to settle down here. This romantic connection ushered a bilateral flow of people between Ireland and the Philippines.

In the 1980s, Martial Law under Ferdinand Marcos sparked an international controversy with the imprisonment of two Irish Columban Fathers.

On 6 May 1983, two Columban priests, the Irish Fr Niall O'Brien and Australian Fr Brian Gore, together with Filipino priest

Fr Vicente Dangan and six lay workers, were wrongly accused of the murders of Mayor Pablo Sola of Kabancalan and his four companions. The trumped-up charges were the result of the group's work with victims of the Marcos dictatorship in Negros.

The group, whose trial and imprisonment earned them the name 'Negros Nine', were held under house arrest for eight months but 'escaped' to prison in Bacolod City, the provincial capital, where they felt they would be safer.

The case received widespread publicity in Ireland and Australia, especially when RTE TV journalist Charlie Bird interviewed Fr. O'Brien in his overcrowded prison cell. Irish government officials arrived in Manila to negotiate with senior officials in the Marcos government for the release of the Negros Nine.

When then U.S. President Ronal Reagan visited Ireland in 1984, he was asked on Irish TV how he could help the missionary priests. The next day, Marcos allegedly received a phone call from the White House. Pressured by the international media and the U.S. government, Marcos relented and offered to pardon the priests and their companions. However, the group refused, as accepting a pardon would imply that they were guilty. Further negotiations between the Irish government eventually led to the charges against the group being dropped. Fr O'Brien and Fr Gore agreed to leave the country, but they made sure that the Philippine government would guarantee protection for the rest of the group. The Negros Nine were finally released on 3 July 1984.

Apart from shining a light on the horrors of the Marcos dictatorship, the incident also marked the beginning of a diplomatic relationship between the Philippines and Ireland.

On 18 June 1990, Mr John Ferris was appointed the Philippine Honorary Consul for Ireland. He was sworn into office by His Excellency Thomas T Syquia at a ceremony held at the Burlington Hotel in Dublin. He would become for the Filipinos not only an exemplary honorary consul for 20 years but a self-appointed watchdog for the cause of Filipinos and other immigrants in Ireland. To this day, his free services as Peace Commissioner are accessible on Facebook and in his Saturday clinic on Capel Street in Dublin. More than 5,000 happy friends on Facebook and clients who attend his clinic get their consular problems eased and many times solved. He has helped thousands of Filipino workers in handling their queries and complaints on employment and visa matters.

The Celtic Tiger Connection

The economic boom from 1998 to 2008, dubbed as the Celtic Tiger period, transformed Ireland from a country of emigrants to one of immigrants. This period saw the most rapid and sudden deployment of nurses, workers and other professionals from non-EEA (European Economic Area) countries to Ireland. Almost overnight, Ireland became a multicultural society with 167 languages being spoken.

In the late 1990s, Ireland chose the Philippines for its nurse-recruitment mission. By 2006, 3,831 Filipino nurses were deployed here, making them the largest group of foreign nurses in Ireland, roughly a fifth larger than the Indians. In a span of seven years (1999–2006), the Philippine Overseas Employment Agency (POEA) listed 6,505 nurses and carers recruited to Ireland to ease the chronic shortage of staff in the country's hospitals and nursing homes. Thousands of Filipino workers and professionals followed suit as they took positions in sectors such as construction, aeronautics, accounting, mining industry, sales, factories, manufacturing and other service-oriented industries. A new batch of domestic helpers, often referred to as 'nannies', was also recruited to meet a big demand.

The wave of migration continued with spouses and children joining Filipino workers under the Family Reunification programme. They were given dependent entry visas, which allowed qualified spouses to take up work, automatically bringing the Filipino population in Ireland from a meagre 300 before the 1990s to over 13,000 today.

A Short-Lived Embassy

On 30 May 2009, Gloria Macapagal-Arroyo, then President of the Philippines, swore in Ariel Abadilla as the country's first full-time resident ambassador to the Republic of Ireland. The appointment followed the announcement by the Department of Foreign

17

whoAffairs of plans to open more embassies and consulates in an effort to reach out and be of service to the ever-growing number of overseas Filipino workers (OFWs). The 2009 initiative saw new embassies established in Ireland, Portugal, Finland, Poland and Syria, and consulates opened in Macau, Chongqing and Chengdu in China.

Ambassador Abadilla presented his letter of credence on 29 June 2009 to Mary MacAleese, then President of Ireland, in a ceremony held at the State Reception Room of Áras an Uachtaráin in Phoenix Park, Dublin. Ambassador Abadilla was accompanied by his daughters, Marienette and Katherine, and Consul General and Minister Hjayceelyn Quintana who also took her post in Ireland. The new ambassador was given military honors at the Aras.

Sadly and unexpectedly, the worst recession in living memory struck the world in 2008 and the Philippine embassy in Dublin closed down in July 2012. A new Honorary Consul, Mark Christopher Congdon, was appointed in October 2012, bringing fresh hope and inspiration to the Filipino community. However, vital embassy services can only be carried out at the Philippine Embassy in London which currently has diplomatic jurisdiction over the Republic of Ireland.

Come what may, the Irish-Philippine connection has come a very long way. By and large, we Filipinos are a happy group of immigrants finding our niche in this country. Our connection is definitely getting stronger as more and more Filipinos receive Irish

18

citizenship. This friendship between our two peoples can only grow as we keep learning about one another. Once a completely alien concept, Ireland for Filipinos has become real—a home away from home.

INTRODUCTION

'Exploring culture is an exciting endeavour, as it involves a never-ending process of discovery. Not only is it the discovery of others, but in that discovery of others, a rediscovery of self.'

—Susan Schneider and Jean-Louis Barsoux,

Managing Across Cultures (2002)

'Who are you?'

'Where is the Philippines?'

'Do Filipinos speak English?'

'Why do you carry Spanish names?'

'Where did you get all those nurses?'

These are just some of the many questions people asked me in my early days in Ireland. While I was happy that people were curious about me, I found myself stammering and struggling with my answers. I was embarrassed to discover that I didn't have much to say about myself, my country and my people. I thought for a while I had to shed off my Filipino-ness to integrate in Ireland. How wrong I was!

As I went through culture shock and struggled to adjust to my new home, I found myself in a never-ending process of self-discovery. I realised that if I wanted to integrate and be confident in another country, I must not only know the other—I must first and foremost know myself.

This reality was made clear during the height of recruitment of Filipino nurses to Ireland during the Celtic Tiger years. Having been here then for more than 20 years, I, along with my husband, was asked by the head of a recruitment company to do a Filipino-Irish enculturation seminar for incoming Filipinos and the Irish staff of hospitals where Filipino nurses were scheduled to work. How and where would I begin? I never had any serious thoughts about my culture when I was in the Philippines.

Describing one's own culture is difficult. It's a bit like asking a fish in water what it's like to swim. Washed up on a beach, the fish quickly recognises the difference but won't be able to describe it. Its immediate objective is to get back into the water. Jim my husband, who had lived and worked in the Philippines for seven years, came to my rescue. An outsider unfettered by preconceptions, he did the job with flying colours.

21

Tomas D. Andres, a Filipino sociologist-anthropologist and author of several books on Filipino culture and tradition, wrote in his book *Effective Discipline Through Filipino Values* (1996):

'The basic skill in the coping process is the capability of an individual to know her/himself, to have integrated with his/her experiences and be able to say, "This is me, my competencies and liabilities, my desires and wants, my needs, my idiosyncrasies."'

'It is in this perspective,' he emphasises, 'where one can size up the dimensions of the other. I do not have control over the other situation, but potentially I have control over my own person, my own culture and upbringing.'

Having been colonised by two western countries, Filipinos had, for a long time, a warped sense of identity. We took pride in being the only Christian, English-speaking country in Asia. Indeed, we are so unlike other Asians in this sense. Chinese, Japanese, Indian, Cambodian and Vietnamese immigrants have such a strong sense of identity, as reflected in their respective languages, cultures and customs. They revel in their uniqueness. Filipinos, on the other hand, tend to lull strangers and themselves into thinking that they're just like westerners.

In the 1960s, many Filipinos came to realise the need to learn about themselves. Andres wrote:

'In his attempt to modernise and develop, the Filipino is faced with a two-fold endeavour: to curve his national identity and to cope with the never-ending change.'

Jose Rizal, himself an immigrant who travelled throughout Europe, once said, *'Ang di marunong lumingon sa pinanggalingan ay di makararating sa paroroonan.'* ('Those who don't know how to look back where they came from will never arrive at their destination.') In the context of cultural integration, it means that unless I know myself and my own culture, I will find it difficult to integrate.

What better way to explore our own behaviour and values than through the lens of an outsider—someone from an alien culture who, unfettered by preconceptions, could point out that the Emperor has no clothes? To borrow from Kipling, 'What know them of the Philippines who only Filipinos know?'

It is with certainty that my exposure to the life and culture of Ireland led me to a better understanding of myself and my own country. We only begin to perceive our culture when we are out of it, confronted by another. 'I understand my country so much better,' said Samuel Johnson, the 18th-century British writer, 'when I stand in someone else's.' Or in the words of French philosopher Jean Baudrillard, 'To open our eyes to the absurdity of our customs is the charm and benefit of travel.'

This is why I've spent my 38 years of living in Ireland on a journey of self-discovery—first, on my own as the only Filipino in Lucan, County Dublin and 23 years later, amidst an Ireland bustling with people of 183 nationalities, including 13,000 Filipinos.

The Purpose of This Book

Often the realisation of the power of culture comes only in retrospect. This book is my way of sharing with the next generation the need to know and understand yourself, to integrate your experiences, and accept all your strengths and weaknesses, your desires and needs, and everything else that makes you who you are

The content of this book is based on my writings published in *Metro Eireann,* the only multicultural newspaper in Ireland, and *Filipino Forum,* where I served as the editor. Both newspapers were set up to help immigrants adjust to and integrate in Ireland during the Celtic Tiger years.

'Who are you?' and 'Why are you here?' were questions being asked on the streets in a place that's now home to a people of a growing variety of colours, languages and cultures. Immigrant workers who initially thought they would only have to adjust to Irish culture realised they would now have to get along with several other cultures in the workplace. Never before had the need for cultural integration been more essential to me, which led me to dig into my identity, and to grasp and explain it through my newspaper columns.

It is important to understand that one's world-view is conditioned by values acquired at a very early age. The world as seen through the eyes of an Australian, a Korean, a German or an American is very different from the way a Filipino sees it. Only by realising that we cannot take our way of seeing the world for granted can we begin to recognise and appreciate how others see the world, and what that might mean for our living together.

When I had my first dinner with Irish people, typical Filipina me wondered to myself, 'Did they run out of spoons? Where's the rice?' We Filipinos grow up thinking that everyone eats with a spoon and has rice with every meal.

Who do we Filipinos think we are? Self-identity is crucial to our understanding of others, those who are 'not like us.' Integrating culturally means we assume the beliefs, practices and rituals of another group without sacrificing our own. The result is a healthy intermingling of different cultures.

On the day he was awarded an honourary doctorate by University College Dublin (UCD), the American sociologist Jeffrey Alexander spoke of the need for immigrants to be visible. He said that there had to a be 'a kind of mutual seduction' and that immigrants needed to create 'dramatic moments' that would help people in the centre of society to 'identify with them.'

Who would make this 'mutual seduction' possible? Who can make us visible in Ireland? Are we bound to follow the fate of our compatriots in America? In spite of the fact that Filipinos have been migrating to the United States since the 16th century and now make up the second largest Asian population in the country, it's still somehow difficult to tell them apart from other nationalities. They are mistaken for Latinos due to their Spanish-sounding names, and for other Asians because of their physical features. Some people even mistake darker-skinned Filipinos for African-Americans. This is the big issue tackled by Filipino-American Brian Ascalon Roley, author of a New York Times 2001 Notable Book of the Year entitled *American Son: A Novel*:

> 'Given our numbers and status as formerly colonized subjects, why are we so invisible to other Americans?'

Our Irish immigration story is fairly new—we've only been in this country for around 50 years. We have a chance to be seen as a unique race and a people that can make a difference while blending harmoniously with other races in Ireland.

How? My aim in writing this book is to raise awareness and to ask questions about our cultural belonging: Who is the Filipino? What does it mean to be Filipino? What is the source of our identity? Where should our attachments and loyalties lie? If the question is a matter of legacy that needs to be passed on and continued, then which aspects of Filipino culture matter?

My casual meetings with Filipino parents over the years also brought up the question of how to raise children the Filipino way in Ireland. As parents, we cannot help but impart our values system to our children. The question thus led to a few more: What are Filipino values? How do they arise from our culture? What are their weaknesses and strengths? How do they differ from universal human values? Are they good or bad? How do we impart them to our children in a foreign land?

In his book *Filipino Values Revisited*, Fr Vitaliano Gorospe advises:

> 'What needs to be done is to understand Filipino values and what the alternatives of acting in accord with them really are.'

Similarly, Tomas Andres wrote:

> 'If a parent wants to effectively discipline, understanding Filipino values is the one vital tools he needs. Disciplining in the Philippine setting without understanding Filipino values is like touring the region without a map. Understanding Filipino values is an integral part of effective discipline.'

As you journey with me through the pages of this book, let us keep these questions in mind.

PART ONE

THE EARLY YEARS (1977–2000)

'Okay, we are different it's true.

And I don't like to do all the things that you do

But here's one thing to think through,

You're a lot like me and I'm a lot like you!'

—Robert Alan Silverstein

1.   A HUNDRED THOUSAND WELCOMES

In their book, *Personality in Nature, Society and Culture* (1953), the anthropologist Clyde Kluckhohn and psychiatrist Henry Alexander Murray made this assertion:

> 'Every man is in certain respects like all other men, like some other men, like no other men.'

I have never been more aware of this reality than in my 38 years of living in Ireland. First, there is the universality of our humanness which is comforting. As human beings, we all go through the stages of birth and dying. And, in between, we grow, laugh, cry and feel pain. Despite our differences in colour, customs and traditions, these shared experiences make it easy for us to enter the lives of other people and allow them into ours.

However, I soon realised that we may not be able to relate to all people in the same fashion. We feel closer to and more at home with people we know well. That's why it was comforting to arrive from the Philippines on 12 September 1977 to my husband's family in Ireland.

I came because I married into the Kennedy family. I met and married Jim in the Philippines where he worked for seven years. Both of us were looking for a new way of being. Jim left the priesthood after 20 years and I left the religious life after ten years. I was in my thirties; he was in his forties. We arrived in Ireland with no job and no home.

But the Irish tradition of *céad míle fáilte* ('a hundred thousand welcomes') was alive and well—a network of relations and friends was there to help us settle down. We were met at the airport and brought home to a good fire and a hot dinner. My 80-year-old mother-in-law travelled all the way by train from Limerick to Dublin to show us support and solidarity. Far from being bitter about losing her priest son to marriage, she welcomed me with great love and generosity. I came to know her as a gentle and kind lady, a good friend, and a mother during our short time together. (She died in 1983). One of her great joys was to see her son get a job and us settle down into a normal family life. She also saw the birth of our two children – Patrick, named after her husband, and Noriana, whose name is Filipino version of her name Nora.

Simple things are beautiful. I was fascinated by fire burning on the hearth. I never thought fire could be kept alive in a sitting room. It was a very warm and welcoming presence especially in winter when we congregated by the fireplace and shared the day's experiences.

In the Philippines, people spend more time out in the open. With temperatures ranging from 26 to 40 degrees Celsius, you'll need air-conditioning and electric fans instead of central heating and fireplaces. Out in the country, you'll find houses built from wood, bamboo, cogon grass and nipa palm to beat the heat and high humidity. When wooden floors became a trend in Ireland, many new Filipino arrivals were disappointed to see these in their rented accommodations, as they would have preferred the warmth of wall-to-wall carpeting.

The weather catches up with you wherever you go. It dictates what you wear, the kind of house you live in and what you eat. I didn't know potatoes made a palatable staple. To us Filipinos, the potato is just another vegetable. Until my arrival in Ireland, I thought everyone ate rice. I was surprised to find out that the Irish eat their main dishes with potatoes instead.

I found myself yearning for Filipino food, especially the varieties of vegetables and fruits grown in the tropics. When I arrived in 1977, there were only apples and oranges in the market, and bananas were four for a pound. Back home, my father would harvest bananas from our yard, and we ate as many as we wanted.

When I was pregnant with my second child, I developed a strong craving for my favourite Filipino fruits—mango, papaya and watermelon. My husband searched every green grocer around and came home empty-handed. Thanks to globalisation, Irish groceries and supermarkets now offer a wide range of exotic fruit from around the world.

As an expectant mother, my first concern was how I'd care for my baby in the cold climate. My first three years in Ireland were weather-beaten days. I arrived in September, and in November came a series of frost, slush, damp, sleet, hailstones, and strong rain aggravated by a few power cuts.

I remember looking out of the window from my maternity bed on that January day in 1978 when my first child was born. I was dazzled by the whiteness of the rooftops, trees and the road. It was the first time I had ever seen snow in my life. I felt I was in fairyland, up until the snow turned to slush and flood. In that weather, I would definitely have to learn how to use hot jars, electric blankets and radiators, and to light a fire, monitor central heating and make loads of cups of tea!

It was shortly after this time too that the malady of culture shock came to the fore. The world-renowned anthropologist Kalervo Oberg defined culture shock as 'a state precipitated by anxiety that results from losing one's familiar signs and symbols.' In short, it is the awful sensation of being a fish out of water.

I now had to learn to use a different currency and a new way of cooking meals. Where before I wore light clothing, now I had to wrap myself up with a coat, hat, gloves, scarf and boots. Culture shock affects even the smallest details of your life.

The realisation that I was in a foreign country gripped me and surfaced in the form of postnatal depression. I found myself constantly weeping for the company of my parents and siblings. The loss of my network of Filipino friends made things even more difficult. Home suddenly felt far, far way.

Oberg and his associates examined the experiences of migrants, asylum seekers, foreign students, returning migrants, missionaries and others whose work took them to other countries. They discovered the startling validity of culture shock and the depressing realities that go with it.

First, there's the strain which comes from the effort to adapt to a new and strange situation. There's a sense of loss and deprivation, brought on by having no available friends or acquaintances, a temporary or permanent change of social status, and a feeling of having deserted one's family. Equally, there's a feeling of inadequacy in a new culture as one notices how they stand out because of their colour, appearance and language.

Cultural differences can lead to loss of identity. You might feel like you've changed from a 'somebody' to a 'nobody' particularly when you're not aware that the culprit is culture shock. Powerlessness arising from isolation can be severe and lead to disorientation if there are negative experiences, such as a migrant being harassed by an employer or an asylum seeker being taunted by locals. A person feels 'de-created' when trust is destroyed.

Culture shock is real. Each person's chaos is unique and cannot be measured by other people. But culture shock can be recognised and acknowledged by the sufferer and can be soothed with a little help from friends.

Fortunately, culture shock is something that eventually wears off. A loving, supportive network of family and friends helps. This could explain why a considerable number of nurses from the Philippines often enter romantic relationships soon after their arrival.

Friends are often behind the decisions that we make. My husband and I moved to Lucan because my sister-in-law Mary and her husband John lived there. They invited us to stay with them for a month as we sorted out the logistics of staying in a new place. Lucan turned out to be the perfect place for us, so we bought a house in Esker Lawns and have stayed there since.

Thirty-eight years on and I'm now well integrated and growing old gracefully. Our two children are happily married in their chosen homes (one in France, and the other in Galway, Ireland). I have become 'more Irish than the Irish,' as they say, and have adjusted to Irish cuisine and many other little nuances of this culture. I love bacon and cabbage, making tea and having a few sips of Guinness.

There were about 3,000 homes in Lucan in 1977. Housing development started in the early 1980s after the Lucan bypass was completed. I thought I would keep my title as the only Filipino in Lucan but in 1999, Ireland's booming economy brought an influx of immigrants, among whom were over 13,000 Filipinos—nurses, engineers, accountants, and workers for different business sectors and services.

The arrival of immigrants has changed Dublin's streetscape. Everyday routines—going to the post office, filling up at the petrol station, shopping, drinking at a pub—have been rendered more colourful by the different nationalities and cultures you encounter as you do them. Of course, you will not miss our own Filipino nurses and carers who form part of the backbone of the country's health services.

The Great Irish Famine in the middle of the 19th century caused Ireland's social history to be dominated by emigration, mostly to the U.S. and Great Britain. This pattern was reversed with the onset of the Celtic Tiger period. Initially, over 3,500 Filipino nurses, carers and nannies arrived en masse here, thanks to the Harney visa. These Filipinos made up one of the biggest groups of foreign nationals to have arrived in Ireland, since the Plantation of Ulster in the 17th century, when English and Scottish Protestant settlers arrived, and in the 12th century, with the Norman invasion.

Tony Feeney, our family GP, states that 20 per cent of his consultations in a day can involve non-Irish people. He tells us in the brochure *Guide to Lucan and Liffey Valley* (2006):

> 'We have been shown the wide world outside of Ireland. The vast majority of these people are happy, integrated and will, no doubt in time, become second-generation Irish.'

2. THE FILIPINA INVASION OF IRELAND: MARRIAGE VOWS UNITE US

'You are you

and I am I

and if by chance we find each other,

it's beautiful.'

—Frederick Perls, 'Gestalt Prayer'

Before the 1970s, the handful of Filipinos in Ireland were mainly members of household staff of foreign embassies. When Tony O'Hanlon from Carlow went to work as a flour mill supervisor in Manila, he met and married Esther Bernandez, and thus started the Filipina invasion rolling when he came back to Ireland with his wife.

The community of Filipino women with Irish husbands built up over the years. Lulu Ledesma from Bacolod and her husband Jack Hynes settled in Dublin; Nora Healy and her husband Pat settled in Co. Clare. Pat's brother Vincent married Alma from Binalbagan and the couple now run a pub in London. Hilary Shannon married

Veronica Castaniego from Negros and set up home in Celbridge.

Pat Keating, owner of one of the best PR companies in Dublin, married Nita from Ilocos Norte. Jim Norton, an accountant, met his wife Angie in Hong Kong, and both became successful entrepreneurs. They run a restaurant, an accounting company and a pharmacy on Capel St.

Genaro Paredes is one of the few Filipino men who married Irish women. He and his wife, Catherine, set up Bahay Kubo, the first Filipino restaurant in Dublin. Antonio Mangaong, a sailor, met Maureen from Rosslare, Wexford, who was assistant manager at her father's pub. When they got married, Antonio took over the management of the pub, from which he has now retired.

There's John Ferris, a wealthy farmer in Castleknock, who met Elby Billote from Pangasinan while he was on holiday in the Philippines. Soon they got married and went home to Ireland where he was later appointed Honorary Consul for the Philippines and served in that capacity for 18 years.

Sean O'Sullivan from Ballycroy in West Mayo found himself enamoured of a tall Filipina he often saw coming out from Sunday mass. Sean told himself, 'She's the woman I will marry.' This is how he met his wife Florita, an au pair. They went on to have five children, the eldest of whom won the prestigious beauty pageant, Rose of Tralee, in 1998. Sadly, Florita died suddenly in her 40s.

As years went by, Filipinas gained a reputation as wonderful housekeepers, nannies and, yes, even as wives. Irish bachelors would turn up at Christmas parties, hoping to find potential Filipina wives. A few dating agencies cropped up to supply a growing demand. Some bachelors failed, a few lucky ones succeeded. I could name some of them—Kerry Vaughan, Christopher Poole and Stevie Cusack.

Kerry travelled all the way to Forbes Park (a plush neighbourhood in Manila) to meet a well-educated, independent woman. Nothing happened. He came home disappointed, only to discover that his future wife was already in Ireland. Kerry started going out with Lutgarda, and several months later, wedding bells tolled for the happy couple in Pampanga.

Christopher Poole, a Quaker, valiantly searched for the girl of his dreams in the Visayas. He went through several frustrating bureaucratic encounters, but in the end, brought home a wife with whom he has now two gorgeous sons. Rosie, his wife, still works in a business establishment in Wexford.

The late Stevie Cusack from Limerick was a sheepdog trial judge in his 40s who was on the lookout for a wife. In one of his travels, he met a Canadian who was married to a Filipina. 'If you want a woman to stand by you,' his Canadian friend declared, 'go to the Philippines.' Inspired by this advice, he went and found his wife Ednalina in Ormoc City, Leyte. The couple set the record for the biggest wedding people had ever seen in Ednalina's hometown! There were a hundred different dishes, and seven lechons (whole roasted pigs) on the top table to feed the entire village. The newlyweds settled in Adare,

Limerick and their union was blessed with five children.

These are just a few of the happy pairings that I know of. With thousands of single Filipinos currently working in Ireland, I'm sure more stories of Filipino-Irish matches are unfolding, and will continue to develop over the years.

My Comfort Blanket

'Do you know of any other Filipinos living here?' I asked my Irish acquaintances soon after my arrival in Dublin. It was shocking to admit that I needed the company of my compatriots to relieve my homesickness.

As a *bagong salta* ('newcomer'), I felt a deep longing to meet and share stories with my *kababayan* ('compatriot'), but nobody was in sight. Despite having a supportive husband and in-laws, I was still homesick. I needed other people with whom I could communicate in Filipino and enjoy a Filipino meal. I needed a security blanket.

I was browsing at a bookshop in the city centre when I spotted Ofelia. We started chatting and ended up at my home where she told me her life story. She was an embassy employee having a stressful time adjusting to her job and Irish life. It was a relief for both of us to have someone to talk to about our difficulties as immigrants.

Several more Filipinos appeared on the scene through the years. As we sat down and shared experiences with one another, it became clear we were suffering from culture shock. There was Marita who couldn't understand her Irish husband's daily drinking habit, Myrna who didn't know how much her husband was earning and whether they had money in the bank or not, Flor who couldn't bear the Irish weather, Marina who couldn't tolerate Irish food, and Tonya who thought she would go crazy because her employer wouldn't allow her to eat rice three times a day! A few found it difficult to communicate with the locals, and there were some who simply wanted to know where they could buy Asian groceries.

Occasionally, some serious problems surfaced as well. Laura, Tessie and Nora escaped from their abusive Saudi Arabian employers and had no idea where to seek help. Sara and Pamela were dismissed and rendered homeless after they complained about unfair wages. At the time, there were hardly any jobs for foreigners in Ireland. Some rich families were allowed to hire domestic workers, and this was the only type of job available to Filipinos.

A group of Filipinos and their families in Ireland in the 1980s

First Filipino-Irish Association

Filipinos in Ireland gradually rose in number. We used to hold parties and meetings in one another's houses, but soon no house was big enough to accommodate 50 or more people. Children were multiplying, and Irish husbands and relations were also keen to attend *Pinoy* parties. We realised that it was time to organise our ever-growing group.

The Filipino-Irish Association (FIA) was born in 1982. The annual Christmas reunions brought us all 'home' in bigger venues where we ate Filipino dishes, danced and sang, and a former missionary priest would say Mass. The FIA was a haven, a place to find solace with kindred spirits. It was a celebration of our being Filipino. Later on, a newsletter called *Bayanihan* ('Working in Unity') provided some social networking facility. The FIA Constitution was written and approved in 1994.

The organisation happily closed in 2000, satisfied that its members had adjusted to and integrated in their respective Irish communities. A new chapter in the history of Filipinos in Ireland was unfolding.

Irish-Filipino Nuptials Breed Beauties

The Rose of Tralee is the most prestigious annual beauty

pageant in Ireland. Held in the town of Tralee in County Kerry, the competition is inspired by a 19th-century ballad about a woman named Mary whose beauty earned her the title of the Rose of Tralee. Some people claim that the song was written by William Pempbroke Mulchinock, a well-to-do Protestant who was in love with his parents' poor Catholic maid, Mary O'Connor.

The festival started in 1959 as part of a campaign to encourage former residents to go back to Tralee. Although it was initially open only to local women, the festival eventually became open to all women of Irish ancestry or heritage.

Luzveminda O'Sullivan, whose parents' romance I mentioned earlier, was the first woman of Filipino heritage to have been crowned Rose of Tralee. Luzveminda won the title in 1998.

Mindy, as she is known among friends, was only ten when her mother Florita died. The young Irish Filipina went on to study biochemistry at Trinity College in Dublin. She was 22 when she became the Rose of Tralee, winning the judges over with her 'beautifully sultry' looks and 'inner radiance', as a 2007 article in the *Irish Independent* described her.

Despite receiving offers to go into full-time modelling, Mindy chose to finish her degree. She now works as a biochemist in a pharmaceutical company in Castlebar, Co. Mayo. She married her hometown friend Patrick Flannelly, and the couple have two sons.

Mindy and her two sons

In 2011, Brisbane-based Tara Talbot became the second Irish Filipino to be crowned Rose of Tralee. Tara is the daughter of Ronan from Dublin and Carmencita from Pangasinan.

The Talbots migrated to Queensland when Tara was five years old; prior to joining the pageant, she returned to Ireland in 2006 and lived between Dublin and Galway for three years.

Tara as the Rose of Tralee 2011

Tara, the bookies' favourite throughout the week of the festival, is the second representative from Queensland to bring the crown back to Australia. As the Rose of Tralee, she received a round-the-world trip worth $40,000, a range of household wear and jewellery from Newbridge Silverware, and a brand-new Renault Megane.

A schoolteacher, she eventually married her long-time Irish boyfriend Fionan Henry in June 2015 in a picturesque wedding in Co. Meath.

3. THE CELTIC TIGER YEARS

Through the 1970s and 1980s, the Filipino community in Ireland thought that their number would stay at around 300. Nobody had foreseen a Filipino exodus to Ireland. The new millennium brought on the economic boom of the Celtic Tiger era, and transformed Ireland into a magnet for immigrants.

Overnight, Ireland became a multicultural society where 167 languages are spoken. The country's dearth of experience in hosting immigrants has led to government policies that are constantly evolving and oftentimes discomfiting to immigrants and their families.

The period was a critical time for Filipinos to adapt and integrate in a new job setting. 'Who are you?' and 'Why are you here?' were questions being asked on the streets in a society not used to seeing various colours, races and creeds. Where they thought they would only deal with the Irish, Filipinos now have to blend with and adjust to several other cultures in the workplace.

The Filipino Forum

The Filipino Forum was a bi-monthly non-profit, non-political news magazine which, at the height of its service, had a readership of about 9,000. It was founded in 2002 by Michael Ancheta who served as Managing Editor. He later relinquished the publication's ownership to me, the Editor. A multimedia expert, Michael pooled all necessary resources, from manpower to organising seminars and liaising with government agencies, to help Filipinos adjust to a new life in Ireland.

The author and other staffers of the Filipino Forum

The Filipino Forum was founded to help uphold the rights and entitlements of Overseas Filipino Workers (OFWs) and consequently those of other immigrants. It provided continuous updates on immigration issues, liaised with immigration agencies such as the Migrant Rights Center (MRCI) and the Irish Immigration Council, and networked with other NGOs. It also provided much-needed assistance on bi-cultural integration through columns and articles on the topic. John Ferris, then Honorary Consul for Filipinos, went out of his way to assist Filipinos in whatever way he could outside of his official duties. He and Michael worked continuously by giving time and expertise to the cause of Filipino immigrants.

PART TWO

DISCOVER THE PHILIPPINES

'My country is the world,

My countrymen are mankind.'

—William Lloyd Garrison,

'Declaration of Sentiments',

The Liberator (1838)

Whenever I visit my hometown, I always notice the strength and positivity of the townfolk. So many of the younger generations have moved away and a majority may not come back, but the people who stayed behind are keeping the fire burning, and are content and happy in themselves.

I envy those for whom identity is straightforward. They were born and will likely die in the same place. For a time, I longed for their sense of belonging while yearning for the excitement and thrill of the outside world. However, I discovered there's a way back home for us who have moved to other places, regardless of how long we have been away.

The next few chapters contain essential information about the Philippines, facts that I researched in my quest to rediscover myself and my Filipinohood.

4. MANY ISLANDS, MANY LANGUAGES

I was born in a little town by the foot of the Sierra Madre mountains in Nueva Ecija in the Central Plain of Luzon. The town was named Papaya after the exotic fruit. A provincial decree later changed the town name to General Tinio in honour of one of our Revolutionary heroes. Even now, however, old folks still call the town Papaya.

My father's job as a district forester meant that our family was constantly moving from one place to another. We set up homes in Cabanatuan City, Zambales, Mindoro, Catanduanes, Marinduque and Manila. However, as the children in our family grew older, our education took precedence. The five eldest children, including myself, had to stay in Manila to concentrate on our studies. I did travel to a few other islands afterwards. Up to now, however, I have only ever been to 20 of the country's 7,101 islands.

His first assignment with the Bureau of Forestry sent my father to the Visayas, where he met and eventually married my mother in Cebu, an island-city in Eastern Visayas, far away from his hometown in Central Luzon. My parents went to my father's home in Nueva

Ecija to live there and raise a family. In the 1930s, marriages between people from different regions of the country were rare and considered kind of taboo. 'Why did you choose someone from so far away?' my grandmother asked my father. 'What's wrong with the local women?'

It was quite a burden on my mother who had not imagined that despite being in her own country, she would have to learn to speak another language and cook the local way and learn the nuances of a different culture. For instance, the Visayan language does not have an equivalent to the Tagalog particles *'po'* and *'ho'* which are used to denote respect. When my mother met her parents-in-law for the first time, instead of saying the usual *'Kumusta po kayo?* ('How are you?') she said, *'Kumusta ka?'*(casual singular form). This caused consternation among her in-laws. *'Susmaria,'* an aunt gasped in horror. 'You Cebuanos do not respect your elders!'

But how true is it really that Cebuanos are not respectful when they're part of a country where respect for elders is sacrosanct? As a teenager vacationing with my Cebuano cousins, I discovered that while the Cebuanos have no 'po' and 'ho', they show respect to their elders—and everyone else for that matter—by speaking in a sweet and lilting, almost apologetic tone. Thus, it is said that Cebuanos never get angry!

Regionalism in the Philippines can be traced to the country's history and geography.

Because the Philippines is an archipelago, many of its provinces are separated from each other by water, while large islands like Luzon and Mindanao are dotted with mountain ranges that separate different land areas. My adoptive town of Iba in Zambales, for example, is separated from the town of Botolan by the Bocao River, a long-winding and wild body of water that swells dangerously during the monsoon season. Because of this river, the people from the two towns spoke two different Zambal dialects!

Regionalism is defined as a tendency to emphasise and value, oftentimes to extremes, the qualities and characteristics of life in a particular place. Here's a classic example: People from the Tagalog region, the Visayas or Pampanga will most likely be stereotyped as spendthrifts, while those from the Northern Provinces are notorious for being incorrigible tightwads. The Visayan region is known for its fertile soil, and historically, Visayans have not had to spend a lot of time tilling the land. Hence they've had more time for leisure and are therefore assumed to be easygoing. Up in the north, on the other hand, the soil is rough, barren and rocky, and requires backbreaking work to produce crops. Hence, for survival, Ilocanos have had to work long, hard hours. Because of unreliable harvests, they've also had to learn to scrimp and save. They are thus known to be industrious and thrifty.

According to historians Teodoro Agoncillo and Oscar Alfonso in *History of the Filipino People* (1968):

'Regionalism is an extension of the closeness of family ties. Invariably, the Filipino believes that the person known to him, no matter how bad, is better than the one unknown to him.'

Our history clearly marks regionalism as an important factor in events that happened centuries ago. Recognising the cultural and language differences among Filipinos, the Spanish colonisers used their policy of 'divide and conquer' to defuse numerous revolts from their disgruntled subjects. It took three centuries for a nationwide revolution to finally happen because regionalism made unification efforts among the different groups of Filipinos a near-impossible feat.

The phenomenon of regionalism is alive and well today. Regional differences are heightened in urban centres. At the University of the Philippines in Diliman, for example, students tend to group themselves according to their regional orientations, which also dictate their choice of residence, network of friends and patterns of organisation. Indeed, Filipinos who hail from the same regions tend to group together wherever they are. As Fr Gorospe stated:

'Regionalism, a trait a migrant had substituted for independence and self-sufficiency, resurfaces as he is confronted with the problems of a strange and complex city.'

When in a strange situation or a foreign place, we tend to seek the support, protection or even just the comfort of a kababayan. Even here in Ireland, Filipino associations are formed based on region—we have groups of Ilocanos, Visayans, Iliganons and

Pangasinenses. As Agoncillo and Alfonso concluded, the Filipino 'does not think in terms of national boundaries, but of regional homogeneity.' Barriers from social status, sex, age and other differences seem to break down as far as *magkababayan* ('townmates') are concerned.

Lost and bewildered in a foreign country, Filipinos tend to seek out other Filipinos for help and support. The more similar they are to each other, the closer the relationship becomes, almost to the point of kinship.

5. A MELTING POT OF PEOPLES AND CULTURES

'Who am I as a Filipino?' is a question that beset me when I arrived in Ireland. It came as a surprise to realise that this question does not have an easy, ready answer.

My identity was a mystery to me. I felt strangely western, sometimes familiarly Asian, always neither fully one nor the other. Who am I?

What gives complexity to my identity is our country's years of colonial experience that introduced foreign ideas which we then adopted in our peculiar fashion. As the travel guide *Lonely Planet* puts it, 'four hundred years in a (Spanish) convent and 50 years in Hollywood' have reshaped Filipino society to the extent that we had believed ourselves to be fully westernised.

As far back as I can remember, English has always been the medium of instruction, from primary school all to way to university. To learn the language, we were not allowed to speak our dialect within the school premises. Some schools even imposed fines on

56

students who were caught speaking the local dialect. Colonialism manifested itself more ardently in the textbooks, most of which were written in English—from grammar and literature, to social studies, history and maths. No wonder then that foreigners are often impressed with how almost everyone speaks and/or understands English. Despite the rigourous English lessons in school, however, we still spoke our own dialect or language at home and on the streets. Thus, majority of Filipinos are at least bilingual, and many speak a variety of dialects and languages

Physically, I can pass for a Chinese, Japanese or Korean. Some Filipinos look South Asian, while others resemble our Southeast Asian neighbours. Our physical features are basically Asian, but there are Filipinos who look white. This is hardly surprising, as we are a mixture of races!

History has made Filipinos a people of many cultures and values. They integrate the Christian values of Europe, and the pragmatic and democratic values of America, as well as the pride and spiritual values of Asia.

The Roots of the Filipino

The Malay

Filipinos are predominantly Malay, and our roots manifest themselves in our ability to adjust to new situations and our desire to be nice, above all things. Filipinos approach trials in life with a smiling countenance, attend to others with decorous gestures, speak

57

cordial words that signify the delicacy of feelings, and are gracious and hospitable.

Filipinos consider frankness a breach of courtesy. Thus, we tend to keep negative comments about other people to ourselves. It's ingrained in our collective psyche that the people who are easy to get along with do well in life.

Readiness to adjust to a new situation and the desire to be nice are the two strongest strains in the Malay character. This pliability had been demonstrated, all through the thousand years of the Malay recorded history: long migrations, painful colonisations, warm weather and a starchy diet. The Malay has always been willing to accept any new concept or a new master and reconcile it to old customs and live with it happily.

A lover of nature and festivities, the Malay tends to live in the here and now. A five-year socio-economic programme or a two-year infrastructure project is too arduous and thus unappealing—it is the carrot, not the stick, that motivates the Malay best.

The Chinese

Filipino culture is predominantly Chinese, and the strongest evidence for this lies in the Filipinos' age-old respect for their elders, such as addressing grandparents as *Lolo* and *Lola*, older brothers as *Kuya* or *Diko*, and older sisters as *Ate* or *Diche*. Fans, slippers and umbrellas are of Chinese origin. Chinese traders started coming to the Philippines in the latter part of the T'ang dynasty (618–907 A.D.), and introduced our ancestors to these now-everyday essentials.

The Chinese mind, a blend of spiritualism and pragmatism, is a substantial part of the Filipino psyche. Patience and perseverance, hardiness and foresight, frugality and thrift have been infused into the Filipino character by the Chinese.

We Filipinos are highly sociable people and consider getting along with our neighbours as a prerequisite to prosperity and happiness. We also subscribe to the ideal of 'sageliness within and kingliness without.' Our high regard for wisdom is evident in our passion for education. We also put a premium on appearances, rituals and etiquette; wealth and class distinctions matter to us too.

Filial piety is another Filipino value that's been imparted to us by the Chinese. Westerners often take our high regard for our elders, especially our parents, as blind obedience, but our respect stems from the fact that our parents have had more experience in life, and therefore should be wise enough to know what's best for their children.

The Heart of the Filipino

Only 2.3% of Asians are Christians, but 85% of Filipinos are Catholic. In fact, we rank sixth in the world in terms of the number of Catholics in the country (39,931,000 out of 94 million people). In comparison, Muslims make up 4.32% of the population; Protestants, 3.06%; indigenous religious sects such as the Aglipayans, 3.5%, and Iglesia ni Kristo, 1.6%; and Buddhists, .09%. Animism, the belief in all things having spirits, is the religion of close to 4 million tribal Filipinos, making up 10% of the population. It has evolved over the centuries and now displays Christian influences.

Spanish colonisers brought Christianity to the Philippines, and along with it, the western concept of political organisation. They enforced Spanish laws, and introduced their language and customs to the Filipinos, as well as their naming system.

Various Filipino dialects have borrowed from the Spanish lexicon. Sunday worship and public holidays are all Spanish influenced. Our mourning and courtship rituals, social customs and standards, even our peculiar mixture of generosity and arrogance— these are all products of three hundred years of Spanish colonisation.

The Mind of the Filipino

When it comes to mentality, ours is very much influenced by America. Unknown to most Filipinos, our relations with the Americans began indirectly in 1792 through the Old China Trade. Of course, we didn't experience full-blown Americanisation until the U.S. occupied the Philippines in 1902. The English language, mass education, public health and road systems are American contributions to Filipino life. America gave Filipinos the mechanics and the techniques of western democracy.

American culture initially gave Filipinos quite a shock. It was a drastic change from the monastic culture imposed by the Spanish to the liberal, glittery world of the Americans. America introduced to the Filipinos the Protestant ethic of rationality, questioning, independent thinking and direct communication.

Who, Then, Is the Filipino?

The Filipino is unique, a product of diverse races and cultures. The Filipino is the legacy of a multi racial mixture of the Malay, the Chinese, the Spanish, the English, the American and the Japanese, all rolled into one. The Filipino is Asian but also European, oriental but also occidental.

However, the evolution of the Filipino as an individual and a culture doesn't end there. The making of the Filipino carries on. They are constantly changing and growing as they journey from one country to another, joyfully embracing new cultures and integrating into new environments, while hurdling the many challenges that come their way. The Filipino is never static—they are a dynamic people, always in motion.

And as more Filipinos cross geographic boundaries and leave their distinct cultural marks on the communities they move into around the world, they continue to prove that among the nationalities of the world, the Filipino is one of the great movers and shakers.

6. THE FAMILY SHARES THE LOAD

My parents came from large families—my mother has eleven siblings, and my father has seven. I remember when two aunts and an uncle on my mother's side stayed with us for four years, during which my parents fed and clothed them, and paid for their school fees. My father made it through college with the financial help of his older siblings and cousins. After he graduated and got a job, he returned the favour by helping pay for his younger siblings' university education. There are nine children in our family, and when four of us went to university in Manila, we stayed with an aunt and uncle free of charge.

This is how the give-and-take system among Filipino families lives on.

The Filipino family always shares the load. Unlike people from many western countries, Filipinos don't get a lot of assistance from the central government. Sadly, Philippine economic and political systems have developed in a way that favours the rich and powerful, and leaves almost nothing for the masses. There are few social welfare benefits, minimal hospital and rural health services, very limited free medical care, no universal pensions for old age and no free education beyond primary school. Members of the family-- sometimes, this means extended family as well—have no choice but to rely on each other to hurdle financial challenges.

For Filipinos, marriage is a 'package deal'—we make a lifelong commitment not just to each other, but to each other's families and relatives as well. Marrying into a Filipino family could easily mean that you would gain a hundred or so new relatives.

Philippine society is familial—the influence of kinship, which centres on the family, is far-reaching. For Filipinos, 'blood is thicker than water', and this belief affects almost all aspects of life—from friendships to work to politics.

Respect and gratitude are the two things that Filipino children are expected to show their parents and elders.

It is unthinkable for Filipinos to make an important decision without consulting their parents first. The Filipino language denotes deep-seated respect for elders, particularly in using 'po' and 'ho' in addressing elders, and referring to them with plural pronouns as a sign of reverence.

Utang na loob ('debt of gratitude') is something that's taken seriously by Filipinos, and our debt to our parents is eternal and immeasurable. This is an alien concept to many westerners, who raise their kids and pretty much 'set them free' once they come of age.

This isn't the case for Filipino children—their parents are their 'creditors' and even in adulthood, they carry the obligation to pay their debt in one way or another.

Filipino familial ties are very strong and are hardly ever broken—not even by marriage, distance or a change in social status. Filipinos who earn a substantial income are obliged to continue supporting their families, even after they get married and start raising their own kids. Those who have moved to other parts of the country are still expected to make time to go home for family gatherings. Filipinos who work abroad are expected to regularly send money to the families—and other relatives—they've left behind.

There are around 4 billion overseas Filipino workers around the world, and these hardworking people are currently supporting families and the Philippine economy through regular monthly remittances. The desire to fulfill their familial obligations is so strong that they tend to send most of their earnings to their families and just keep a little for themselves, especially in the first few years of separation.

According to Florio Arguillas in his thesis 'The Transnational Families of Filipino Nurses in Ireland in the Midst of an Emerging Philippines-Ireland Migration System', here are some reasons Filipino nurses in Ireland cite for sending remittances:

'It is part of our culture.'

'That's how we are.'

'It is in our nature.'

However, if one probes deeper, we see that majority of them aim to improve the recipients' lives by making them self-sufficient and financially independent. One interviewee said:

> 'My brother asked for money so he could start an internet café business. Initially, I bought ten computers, but it turned out it wasn't enough, so I added ten more, and then added seven more. Right now there are 27 computers in his internet café. The business is thriving, so I won't have to give him more.'

Vivian, a married nurse said,

> 'I put up a bakery for my mother. It is a big bakery! I don't have to worry about them now. I don't send remittances to them anymore!'

Most of the nurses Arguillas observed were investing or at some point in the past had invested in the human capital of close or extended relatives. They contributed to the education of their nieces, nephews and cousins, and did not stop sending money until these relatives got their diplomas and were settled in their jobs.

7. WE ARE NOT SPANISH!

'What's in a name?

That which we call a rose

by any other name would smell as sweet.'

—William Shakespeare,

Romeo and Juliet (II, ii, 1-2)

The sense of personal identity and uniqueness that a name gives a person is at the heart of why names interest us, and why they are important to us as individuals and communities.

When trying to construct our family tree, my father couldn't trace the source of our surname 'Benavidez'. Nobody among our relatives knew the answer either. The mystery would not have been solved had we not come across the *Alphabetical Catalogue of Surnames* online.

The book (*Catálogo alfabético de apellidos* in Spanish, *Alpabetikong Katalogo ng mga Apelyido* in Filipino) is a list of surnames published in the Philippines and other territories of Spanish East Indies in the mid-19th century.

Consider some of the names from the catalogue: Abesamis, Abelardo, Arenas, Asencio, Avellaneda, Averilla, Azucena, Aquino, Arestorenas, Abadesco, ,Abalena, Adriatico, Agravante, Aguilar, Aguirre, Alba, Almeda, Alonzo, Alvarez, Amando, Amatorio, Amos, Anastacio, Alcala, Benavidez, Buenavista, Bandril, Bantillo, Baquiran, Barcelona, Barrios, Baterina, Bautista, Bedana, Beltran, Bernaldez,Bernardino, Borbon, Borja, Borromeo.

Looking at these, you would think that the people who bear them are Spanish or Latino. However, less than 5% of Filipinos have Spanish ancestry. So why are we the only Asian country where most people carry Spanish surnames?

After the Spanish invaded the Philippines, many Christianised Filipinos chose surnames such as de los Santos, de la Cruz, del Rosario and Bautista for their religious significance. These surnames are fairly common, even today.

Other Filipinos took inspiration from famous Filipino chieftains such as Lacandola and Lontoc in their choice of surnames. What made things more complicated was that many people within the same family had different surnames. Colonial authorities found that this randomness hindered their efforts to conduct a proper census of the archipelago's inhabitants and to collect taxes.

On 21 November 1849, the Spanish administration of the Philippines, under the authority of Governor-General Narciso Claveria, decreed a systematic distribution of family names and the implementation of the Spanish naming system. In Zambales, for example, heads of families in the 14 towns were named alphabetically from north to south starting from Iba, the capital. If your family name started with A or B, people would know that you came from the northern part of the province; people whose surnames began with any letters of the alphabet from C to N were from the southern towns.

Fortunately (or unfortunately, as some would think), the Claveria decree didn't reach every nook and corner of the Philippines, which is why several indigenous Filipino names have survived. Thus, we have surnames like Abao, Abat, Abay, Abog, Akiaten, Alinsangan, Ambat, Bacud, Bacol, Bacani, Bagang, Bagsit, Bagtas, Batad, Balutan, Balagtas, Camat, Camut, Caligtasan, Dampay, Dasal, Dapitan, Malinaw, Maligaya, Marapat, Malicsi, Paras, Panupat, Panganiban and Talucad.

Some Aeta tribes have continued naming their descendants after a basic characteristic or quality of a person, e.g., Mabilis, Pilay, Kirat, Pandak, Tagaluas, Tagahulo, Payat, Taba.

Some names are not flattering to their owners but, for obvious reasons, most of the native names that have survived are those that express the positive or powerful qualities of people. There is strength and fierceness in names like Macaraeg (able to win), Catacutan (to be feared), Panganiban (aware of danger), Agbayani (Ilocano, to be heroic) and Mangubat (Cebuano, to fight). There is defiance in Tagalog names like Dimaapi ('cannot be oppressed'), Dimayuga (unshakeable), and Lacanilao (Lakan-ilaw), or 'noble light'.

Modern Myths

Claveria's decree is at the root of some myths and misunderstanding that we have today about Filipino names. Some people believe that the Spaniards forced Filipinos to give up their own names and assume Spanish names, but this is not true. The catalogue listed all kinds of names that were collected from all over the Philippines. The purpose of the catalogue was not to get rid of native names but to set up a civil register so that the government could keep track of the Filipino population for tax collection, law enforcement and church records. To do that, Claveria needed all Filipino families to have surnames. The origin of the surname did not matter as long as each family member had the same one.

Another myth is that having a Spanish surname means having some Spanish ancestry. Some Filipinos assume, and in some cases even claim, that one of their ancestors bore children with a Spaniard.

The truth is that for most of the Spanish era, there were very few Spaniards in the Philippines. In most provincial towns, the only Spaniard was the local friar. According to the 2000 census, 95% of Filipinos have pure Malay heritage.

Although mestizos (mixed-race people, particularly those who are half-Spanish or half-American) are extremely influential in Filipino society, most estimates put the number of Filipino mestizos at no more than 3% of the entire population, and only about half of those are Spanish mestizos, who are based mainly in Manila and Cebu.

Whatever their origin—Spanish, Malay or native—most Filipinos today possess family names that only date back to 1849, and for that, they can thank or blame Claveria's catalogue.

8. RICE IS OUR LIFE

I grew up on the paddies of Nueva Ecija, the rice granary of the Philippines. The rice fields were our playground, and harvesting and selling rice was our first workshop on setting up our own business. At a young age, we learned the art of planting, winnowing and pounding rice, and the value of this grain was inculcated in our daily existence.

'Rice is life,' my father would remind us, 'and you must learn how to conserve life.'

Rice is one of the world's most important food crops. It is the staple food for more than half the world's population and 90% of Asians. Rice farming is the largest single use of land for producing food. This crop is grown on 250 million Asian farms, most smaller than one hectare, and is the single most important source of income for rural people. It is the single largest food source for the poor.

Rice is life for Asians, the cornerstone of our civilisation. It's not just a supplement to the meal; it **is** the meal. Rice is so central to life that it inspires reverence among those who grow and eat it.

The sacredness of rice stems from how the people who have grown it have survived centuries of crop failures, blight, war and drought.

Rice is a crop that is grown in paddies flooded by water from the monsoon rains. No rain means no rice, and no rice means no life. In Japan, Korea and China, the most meaningful gift you can give a friend is a set of rice bowl and chopsticks. Even the cheapest mass-produced rice bowl is adorned with an ornate pattern.

There is something spiritual about the act of planting rice itself. Japanese farmers are known to pray at dawn before they begin ploughing their fields. Some Filipino farmers pray novenas for rain.

A Japanese theologian, Masao Takenaka, wrote a book with a provocative title, *God Is Rice: Asian Culture and Christian Faith*. In this contemplative book, Takenaka asserts that to an Asian, rice is the symbol of God's gift of life. God is life, rice is life; therefore, for us Asians at least, it's more appropriate to consider God as rice instead of as the bread of life.

A bountiful rice harvest is a cause for celebration. We hold a *pipigan* ('rice-pounding party') where we celebrate the first harvest of the season by feasting on the famous *guinataang malagkit* (sticky rice cooked in coconut milk). Harvest time sees granaries swell with the year's bounty and dining tables laden with varied *kakanin* (rice cakes) such as *putong puti, suman, biko* and *kutsinta*.

When the price of rice suddenly shoots up, we know that the

country is in trouble. This is not just a food crisis, it is a threat to our cultural heritage.

Rice is incorporated into our religious beliefs. We have rice gods and patron saints to guard the granaries, and rituals for rain and good harvests. Across the region, eating sticky rice together is seen by some as a way of keeping kin and friends together. We serve rice noodles (*pancit bihon*) at birthday parties to wish the birthday celebrants a long life.

Rice is incorporated into various art forms. Some of our folk dances replicate the planting and winnowing of rice. The world-famous *Pahiyas* festival in Lucban, Quezon revolves around making and displaying the incredible *kiping*—colourful, festive decorations made from glutinous rice paste.

Our language is rich with rice-related words: *punla* (seedling), *uhay* (young plant), *palay* (harvested grain), *bigas* (polished rice), *sinaing* (boiling rice), *kanin* (cooked rice), and *lamig* or *bahaw* (leftover rice).

We also have several rice-themed sayings and expressions.

'Marami ka pang bigas na kakainin' ('You still have a lot of rice to eat') is a reminder to young people or beginners that they still have a lot to learn. In the dark days of Martial Law, militant farmers coined the phrases, *'Bigas, hindi bomba'* ('Rice, not bombs') and *'Bigas, hindi bala'* ('Rice, not bullets') as rallying cries against the government for turning rice fields into battlefields, and starving farmers and their families.

Among Filipinos at the base of the socio-economic triangle, you will often hear this plea: '*Kahit pambili man lang ng bigas.*' There's so much pathos in these words that it's impossible to translate them properly into English. For Filipinos, rice is first on the list of essential items. Forget the *ulam* ('main dish'). For well-fed Filipinos, rice is just another item on the food-shopping list. But for those who have nothing, rice, and only rice, is what will make them survive the day.

9.   WE ARE WHAT WE EAT

What is the best way to tackle racism? Answer: Filipino food.

In a public forum in Killarney, Co. Kerry in 2006, asylum seekers and migrant workers were told that they could integrate with their local community through participation in local sports, church groups and social clubs.

This, of course, is not a problem for Filipinos. We are naturally sociable and gregarious, eager to share ourselves—especially our food—with family, friends and co-workers. At meal times in hospitals and other places where Filipinos work, their colleagues often look forward to seeing their *baon* ('packed meal'), as Filipinos often bring enough food to feed a large group of people.

The high esteem in which Filipinos hold their food is encapsulated by the commonly expressed invitation, 'Let's eat!' Food is a comfort blanket for Filipinos and to be without it is a cause for panic. Filipinos always have to have some food on them to ward off hunger wherever they may be.

76

In Ireland, you're considered poor if you can't afford to buy drinks. In the Philippines, you're poor if you can't afford to eat rice three times a day—breakfast, lunch and dinner. We also have sticky rice cakes for *merienda* ('snacks') and dessert. Plus, there's the traditional *pulutan* or appetiser that accompanies pre-dinner drinks. Our national obsession with food has led a a bewildered Irishman to say, 'Filipinos are always eating everywhere, even in the workplace!'

Their love for food and social gatherings has made it easier for Filipinos to integrate into Irish society. They invite their neighbours to family celebrations and Philippine Independence Day events, and are ready to contribute to potluck meals in many a community and church gatherings. The *adobo* and *pancit* are taking centre stage and integrating well on Irish buffet tables. Lechon, or whole roast pig, is the definitive fiesta dish now visible in Ireland. Since the arrival of Filipinos in the country, the demand for whole raw pig rose substantially, owing to Filipinos who cannot have a party without lechon! Some supermarkets now display whole raw pigs on their butcher shelves.

What Is Filipino Food?

In her book, *Philippine Food and Life*, Gilda Cordero-Fernando asks:

> 'Is Filipino food the *adobo* which has a Spanish name, yet covers chicken, pork, vegetables or even seafood stewed in vinegar and

garlic, and is thus unlike any Spanish *adobado*? Or is it *pancit*–noodles of many persuasions, found on many table and utilising local ingredients, yet obviously of Chinese origin? Or would it be *sinigang*—the sour broth allied to similar Southeast Asian soup-stews—that's cooling in hot tropical weather? Could it even be the omnipresent fried chicken—sometimes marinated in vinegar and garlic before it is fried? Or *arroz caldo*—chicken congee that is popular even on airlines as comfort food? Could it be all the above? Where did it all begin, where did it come from and how did it develop?'

Filipino culture has always been based on our country's lush environment, but the foreigners who came to our islands, either for trade or conquest, inadvertently left their marks on many aspects of our daily life as well.

Our storied past and Mother Nature's largesse combined and evolved to produce Filipino cuisine as we know it today.

Many Chinese traders who came to our shores decided to stay, and brought with them their culture and cuisine, which greatly influenced ours—thus we have pancit (Hokkien for 'something quickly cooked') or noodles, *lumpia* (spring rolls), *siopao* (steamed filled buns) and *siomai* (dumplings).

When the Spanish arrived in the 16th century, they brought with them both their cuisine and that of Mexico, through whose vice-royalty they governed the Philippines. They introduced dishes that were meant for the elite, ruling class, and for which many ingredients were not locally available. Paella, a simple rice dish originally prepared by Spanish farmers, became a more elaborate and luxurious mixture of meat, seafood and vegetables. *Relleno,* which literally means 'stuffed' in Spanish, also became a popular addition to the Filipino cuisine—and chicken relleno became a Christmas dinner feature, but the most popular type is *bangus*, the silvery milkfish that's notoriously difficult to debone.

When *pansiterias* ('noodle shops') opened in the 19th century, Chinese dishes were given Spanish names for the ease of the clientele, thus *comida China* ('Chinese food') included *arroz caldo* (rice and chicken gruel) and *moresqueta tostada* (fried rice).

The Americans introduced convenient food and cooking techniques to Filipinos—using a pressure cooker, precooked meals, making sandwiches and salads, burgers, fried chicken and grilled steaks. Over time, French, Italian, Middle Eastern, Japanese, Thai and Vietnamese influences added to the Filipinos' culinary repertoire.

This is what Filipino food is—a constantly evolving story of our land and the people who populated it, of new settlers and their histories, and the way native Filipinos embraced these new people's cultures and cuisines and made them uniquely Filipino

With patience and goodwill, we will eventually see the indigenisation of Filipino food in Irish cuisine, paving the way for integration and better understanding. It will prove once again that the way to a people's heart is through their stomach.

10. WE ARE A COUNTRY OF NURSES

Nobody among the original Filipino community in Ireland ever thought that someday, the country would be flooded with migrants from the Philippines. Thanks to the Harney visa, which made it possible for skilled foreign workers and their families to enter Ireland, nursing became the most dominant Filipino occupation in Ireland in the first decade of the millennium. Filipino nurses gained a reputation for their unique way of caring for and sensitivity towards their patients, something that received coverage from the Irish media and from Health Service Executive (HSE) personnel themselves.

Here's just some of the positive feedback Filipinos have received about the quality of their nursing work:

> 'Clinical competence, a good heart, a helping hand and a pleasant personality make Filipino nurses stand out. The children and families of Ireland are indebted to them for their commitment to children's nursing.'

> —Lorcan Birthistle, Chief Executive,
> Our Lady's Children's Hospital, Crumlin

'Nurses from the Philippines commenced employment in Connolly Hospital in 2001.... and currently there are 129 nurses on staff. Their contribution ... has been immense in that they have enabled the Nursing Service to have appropriate staffing levels to maintain a quality service. A number of staff have been promoted and are excelling in their management role.

—Mary Walshe, Hospital Manager,
Connolly Hospital

'Our Filipino colleagues integrated well into our hospital and their personal and professional nursing experience has continued to deliver a caring service to our patients over the years.

—Mary Mills, Director of Nursing,
Cork University Hospital

Data from the Philippine Overseas Employment Agency (POEA) reveal that between 2000 and 2006, the Philippines sent a total of 3,512 nurses to Ireland, 82 per cent of whom were women. In 2002, a new group of Filipino workers hired directly from Malaysia and Singapore arrived in Ireland to work mostly as nannies, as there's no work permit category for domestic workers. From 1999 to 2006, the Philippines deployed 6,505 workers—54 per cent of whom are nurses, and 69.76 per cent are women.

The Philippines is now a major player in the international market for nurses. In 2000, data from the POEA revealed that the

81

Philippines exported nurses to over 60 countries. In 1998, half (49.3 per cent) of the registered nurses trained in the Philippines were working abroad, 8.9 per cent were employed locally as nurses, and the remaining 41.8 per cent were either unemployed or working in non-nursing professions.

Filipino nurses are in demand abroad because of their skills and their caring attitude. There's also less of a communication barrier with Filipino nurses—they speak English, and have received an education that's geared towards both local and foreign patients.

A Brief History of Migration

The Philippines is one of many labour-exporting countries in the world, but Filipino migrant workers are not a recent cultural phenomenon. In the beginning of the 20th century, thousands of Filipinos were shipped out to work in the plantations of Hawaii, the canneries of Alaska and the farms of California. But it was the deteriorating economy in the 1970s that led to a significant number of Filipinos being forced to find jobs abroad.

President Marcos and his successors were only too happy to send overseas contract workers (OCWs), as they were called then, to relieve the pressure of unemployment and increasing levels of poverty. The export of Filipino manpower was supposed to be a temporary stop-gap measure, but our country has become reliant on the income brought in by our hardworking OFWs.

In 2000, the level of unemployment in the Philippines ranged from 9 to 11 per cent and foreign debt was at $50 billion. The continued exportation of labor is a source of much-needed dollar reserves. Our country is part of the global economy, exporting goods mostly to the U.S. However, if you compare the 2006 figures for the remittances from OFWs ($12.7 billion) and the country's total export earnings ($2.3 billion—a mere 18% of the total remittances), you'll see why OFWs and their earnings are still the single most important source of dollar reserves in the Philippines.

Push and Pull Factors

The main pull factor for Filipino nurses is, of course, the shortage of nurses in America, Ireland and many other developed countries. Deciding to leave one's homeland is always heart-wrenching, but American salaries are a large incentive. A nurse in the U.S. can earn $3,000 a month, while a doctor in the Philippines earns $400 a month and a nurse, $200. According to the Department of Health, in 2000 there were around 27,160 nursing posts in public and private hospitals and clinics, as well as educational institutions. This is a much lower number than the actual number of qualified nurses in the country.

Conditions in Ireland

In the 1990s, the Irish economy experienced an unprecedented growth. The country's Gross National Product (GNP) registered a sustained average growth of 7.5 per cent from 1994 to 1999, while its Gross Domestic Product (GDP) posted an average growth of 8.4 per cent within the same period. Unemployment rate was low, and so was inflation. This economic boom swiftly transformed what once was a traditional emigrant-sending nation into an immigrant-receiving one.

What made this more remarkable was that just seven years prior to 1994, Ireland's economy was in crisis, with the national debt at 125% of the GNP. The situation was so dire that in January 1998, *The Economist* described Ireland as the 'poorest of the rich', the rich being Northwest European countries.

The economic growth led to an increased demand for skilled workers, which could not be fully met by the local labour force. The speed at which the economy improved left the education sector with little time to turn out Irish graduates with skills needed in the construction, chemical and IT industries.

All over Europe, fertility levels were declining and populations had begun aging. Ireland was no exception. The declining fertility levels in Ireland were partly attributed to the legalisation of contraceptives in 1979. While the decline in fertility had resulted in a demographic dividend that helped give birth to the Celtic Tiger

84

(Donovan and Murphy, 2013), it worked against specific skills sectors like nursing, which relied on a pool of young, mostly female workers, as the economic boom provided Irish youth with other career options.

Nursing Shortage in Ireland

By the mid-1990s, the Irish health care sector was experiencing an acute shortage of nurses. Not only was the recruitment of students for general nursing courses declining (Wells and McElwee, 2000), many nurses, disillusioned with how they were undervalued and overworked by the health service, were also leaving for other countries. Add to this the Irish public's perception of nursing as a lowly profession and the government's failure to heed earlier calls to address the nursing shortage, and the result was the curtailment of health services. Some beds had to be closed, as in the case of the Mater hospital in October1999. Elective surgeries were postponed or cancelled. There were long waits at surgeries, health centres and hospitals.

The crisis finally reached a point where it could no longer be ignored by the government. The best solution was to recruit English-speaking nurses from other countries. When recruiting nurses from within the EU didn't quite make up for the shortage, the government expanded the search to non-EEA countries.

Filipino nurses were an obvious choice as their skills were already recognized in the U.S. and the UK. As the Secretary General of the Department of Health and Children said at the Committee of Public Accounts hearing on the subject: 'There is a ready welcome for [Filipino nurses] in the Irish system.'

The Professional Regulation Commision of the Philippines was asked to provide the An Bord Altranais (Irish Nursing Board) with certification that attests to the qualifications of Filipino nurses, and after a brief delay in sorting the certification out, Filipino nurses started arriving in the second quarter of 2000.

Motivations of Nurses for Working in Ireland

Filipino nurses have various reasons for opting to work in Ireland, and these reasons varied depending on whether nurses were recruited directly from the Philippines or were already working in another country.

Those who were hired from the Philippines wanted a better work environment and a higher pay. They cited unsatisfactory working conditions at home, including disproportionate staffing ratios, lack of opportunities for professional development, and low pay.

Several nurses who were hired directly from Saudi Arabia felt that Irish culture would suit them better than Saudi Arabia's restrictive one, which requires women to have minders when they go out shopping, and forbids them from talking to men outdoors.

While the demand for them may have waned in the U.S., Filipino nurses are still popular in many countries. Filipino nurses working for the National Health Services (NHS) in England drew international attention in 2000 when Prince Philip, while touring a new cardiac centre in Bedfordshire, turned to a Filipino nurse and said, 'The Philippines must be half-empty—you're all here running the NHS.'

According to a POEA report in 2004, there were 90,000 Filipino nurses around the globe from 1992 to 2004. The Philippines is considered a leading supplier of nurses to developed countries, as Filipinos comprise 25% of nurse migrants in developed countries (Estella, 2005). A 2007 article in the *Philippine Star* stated that around 83% of nurses working in the United States were Filipinos.

11. WE ARE THE FOURTH LARGEST ENGLISH-SPEAKING COUNTRY IN THE WORLD

'**D**o Filipinos speak English?' was a question I would often get asked in my early days in Ireland. Not everyone knows that the Philippines in the fourth largest English-speaking country in the world, after the U.S.A., the United Kingdom and India. This isn't surprising at all, with Filipinos being taught from an early age to speak, understand and write English.

My mother sang English lullabies to help me sleep when I was a baby. The earliest rhymes and games I learned—'I have two hands' and 'I spy'—were my early introduction to the English language. By the time Filipino children enter primary school, they will have built a vocabulary of English words that include parts of the body, names of animals and objects, verbs and nursery rhymes, as well as answers to questions such as 'What's your name? and 'Where do you live?' They will also have had constant exposure to media—there are plenty of English-language TV and radio shows, music and films in the

Philippines.

Doray Espinosa writes in *Global Issues in Languages* (1997):

'For most middle and upper class Filipino children, English begins at home with adults who use English or through snatches of English words and phrases heard over the radio and on TV. To the Filipino child or, at least, one who has grown up in a home where English is often heard and spoken, English is not an alien tongue. Filipino children may not understand the nuances of the English language, but it's there and it's theirs to manipulate. English is familiar and, better yet, user-friendly.'

The Philippines was a Spanish colony for 333 years, but in 1898, Spain ceded our country to the U.S., which then colonised us for the next 50 years. By the time the Americans left, Filipinos had adopted the American form of government, and English was one of our country's official languages.

The Thomasites were a group of around 540 American teachers who arrived in the Philippines on 21 August 1901. Their goal was to establish a new public school system, teach basic education and train Filipino teachers, with English as the medium of instruction. The Spanish introduced public schools to the Philippines in 1863, but it was the Thomasites who expanded and improved the system.

In the decades after the U.S. granted the Philippines its independence in 1946, the connection between the two countries has undergone many changes. But English—or Philippine English, as our variant of the language is known—continues to be an integral part of our culture, whereas Spanish is now spoken only by a few.

Consider the statistics cited in *Philippine English: Linguistic and Literary Perspectives* by Ma. Lourdes Bautista and Kingsley Bolton:

'The latest results from a Social Weather Stations (2006) survey suggest that some 65 per cent of the population claim the ability to understand spoken and written English, with 48 per cent stating that they write English, but with only 32 per cent reporting that they speak the language.'

Our fluency in English is such that many students from countries such as South Korea, Iran, Brazil and Russia go to the Philippines to learn English. Compared to the UK, the U.S. and Australia, the Philippines offers colleges and universities that teach English at much cheaper rates. The fact that Filipinos speak with a clear American accent is also appealing to overseas students.

Our proficiency in American English has also made the Philippines a hub for call centres that cater mostly to U.S. markets.

12. FILIPINO WOMEN AND MEN HAVE EQUAL RIGHTS

'Who are the best-educated foreigners coming into Ireland?'

Fintan O'Toole of the *Irish Times* sought the answer to this question and came up with the following:

'It's the Filipinos and the Indians. More than 80 per cent of those coming here from the Philippines who are women, and more than 70 per cent of Indians, have a third-level education, compared with half of the Germans, Italians and Dutch.'

When the first batch of Filipino nurses arrived in Ireland, some Irish people asked in disbelief: 'Where did all these Filipino nurses come from?' For so long, the Irish media only reported on poverty and destitution in the Philippines. What they did not know is that the Philippines produces highly educated people, including nurses and doctors competent enough to work in other countries.

The Irish HSE recognised Filipino nurses' abilities and propensity for learning by awarding some of them with MA scholarships, which would help them not just to upgrade their qualifications but also to eventually teach at Irish nursing schools.

As of 2016, the literacy rate in the Philippines is 96.34%, giving it a ranking of 55 out of 160 countries, according to figures released by the UNESCO Institute for Statistics (UIS). Basic literacy—the ability to read and write—is almost universal in the Philippines.

What's most significant about these statistics is the comparison of literacy levels among Filipino men and women. Whereas the world literacy rate for men is 90% and that for women is 82.7%, in the Philippines, male literacy is at 95.8% and female literacy is at 96.8%. This is an impressive figure, especially for a developing country like ours.

It has been suggested that Filipino women enjoy more rights in their country than their western counterparts do in theirs. This isn't really surprising, as pre-colonial Philippine society was largely matriarchal. Pre-Hispanic records showed that barangays had male and female leaders—most notable of whom were Princess Urduja and Queen Sima. The *babaylan* ('priest or shaman') were revered members of pre-colonial society, and most were women.

At present, women maintain a very high profile in public life— we've had two women presidents, and our Senate, Congress and courts, down to the smallest barangay, have benefitted from the presence of women leaders. We have women doctors, lawyers, scientists and bankers, and women also dominate the fields of education, pharmacy and dentistry. Filipino women generally acquire more formal education than males at every level—they earn nearly two-thirds of the master's degrees and about 80 per cent of doctorates.

Even in familial settings, no one can question the role that women play. Who holds the purse and takes charge of the children's education? The mother. Who traditionally pays for the wedding expenses? The groom. Do Filipinas need a dowry to marry? Never.

Filipino girls generally grow up with a strong self-image. While still young, they are given more responsibilities within the family than their brothers. In both urban and farming families, wives and husbands have equal responsibilities. Family property is divided equally among all children, and women retain ownership even after marriage.

In one of our creation myths, Malakas, the first man, and Maganda, the first woman, were found in the internodes of a bamboo, a symbol of the equality between men and women. Sexual equality is likewise reflected in our national language. Filipino doesn't distinguish between male and female genders; instead, we have one pronoun, *siya*, to refer to a person, regardless of gender.

In 1950, the Civil Code of the Philippines was enacted under Republic Act No. 386. The Civil Code was modelled after the Spanish *Codigo Civil*, and thus contained some articles that were prejudiced against women. For instance, it allowed a man to dispose of conjugal property without his wife's consent.

In 1987, President Corazon Aquino signed into effect the Family Code of the Philippines, which amended several articles in the old Civil Code. The Family Code allows a woman to engage in business transactions without the prior consent of her husband and to dispose of property which she owned prior to her marriage. It also prevents the husband from getting rid of conjugal possessions without the consent of his wife.

The 1987 Philippine Constitution also protects Filipino women. According to the Constitution, marriage to a foreigner does not strip a Filipina of her citizenship unless, through her own act or omission, she is deemed to have renounced it. Her children are also considered natural-born citizens of the Philippines by virtue of her own citizenship.

Filipinos use the phrase 'under the *saya* ('skirt')' to make fun of a man who gets bossed around by his wife. But most Filipino men are happy for their wives to take the lead when it comes to managing their families, from deciding how their money gets spent to choosing which clothes everyone in the family should wear. This also translates to many businesses, and women managers are not a rarity in the Philippines. Indeed, Filipino women tend to be very active and frequently more aggressive than men in social and economic activities.

Despite this, however, Filipino women still tend to be fetishized by some western men who believe that Asian women are servile, meek and eager to please. What these men don't realise is that

94

underneath the veil of graciousness, humility and sweetness that many Filipino women wear is a fascinating combination of intelligence, determination and shrewdness. This is what distinguishes them from western women—they have mastered the art of hiding their strength by putting on a soft, coy façade.

This is not to say that Filipino society is perfect in its attitude towards women—there are still plenty of men who objectify women and think that a woman's place is only in the home. However, Filipino children are constantly exposed to environments where women are leaders, from schools to workplaces to politics and the media. We are not lacking in role models when it comes to Filipino women in leadership roles.

This is most likely the reason many women in the Philippines have never been aggressive feminists. It's not because we don't believe in equal rights for women and men; it's just that most of us are already benefitting from the equality that women in other countries are still fighting for.

13. A CHRISTIAN COUNTRY IN ASIA

My thoughts always drift towards home during Holy Week. The most revered liturgical season among Catholics is Lent or *Cuaresma*, the 40-day period from Ash Wednesday to Easter Sunday, which commemorates the Passion of Christ—His life, death and resurrection.

Traffic on Philippine roads reaches nightmarish proportions as people take advantage of the four-day holiday that begins on Maundy Thursday and ends on Easter Sunday. This is the time for families to get together, not just to pray, but to celebrate and catch up on one another as well. The four-day weekend is normally a whirlwind of visits to churches and socialising with relatives and friends.

Filipinos are a religious people who turn to faith in times of trouble. However, we are not dogmatic; rather, we see religion as a way of life with rituals that provide continuity and moral purpose, and contribute to communal unity. Elements of pre-colonial tribal belief absorbed into Catholicism have resulted in a form of 'folk Catholicism' that manifests itself in various homespun observances.

For instance, you'll often find a *manghihilot* ('folk healer') reciting verses from Catholic prayers mixed with native rituals. It's also common for anyone opening a business not just to ask a priest to bless their business premises, but to also scatter rice around for good luck. Indeed, superstition is an integral part of our Catholic faith.

Tourists are amazed at the variety of processions, rituals and ceremonies to watch and participate in during Holy Week. For Filipinos, these are audio-visual presentations of the Christian faith— an annual reminder of the life, death and resurrection of our Lord Jesus Christ.

During Holy Week, you'll find throngs of people visiting famous images of Christ in churches around the country, and penitents flogging their backs to a bloody mess or volunteering to be 'crucified.' The Church does not encourage such fanaticism, but, as any visitor would soon realise, Filipinos practise their faith in a very different way.

Paete, Laguna: Holy Week Processions

In Paete, the start of Holy Week is marked with the commemoration of Jesus' triumphant entry into Jerusalem with the *Payakpak*. This Palm Sunday procession begins at Ermita Chapel, where the priest blesses palm fronds held by churchgoers as they

97

head to the beautiful church of Santiago de Apostol. As the priest makes his way to the altar, women drape shawls on his path

In the five days leading to Good Friday, hordes of people pay their respects to a centuries-old *Santo Sepulcro,* a wooden statue of Jesus' dead body, by kissing his exposed hands and feet. On Holy Wednesday, the statue is given a ritual bath, followed by the start of the *pabasa* (the Passion of Christ recited in song), which goes on until Good Friday.

On Good Friday, the *Siete Palabras,* a meditation on Christ's last words on the Cross, is held from noon until 3 p.m., after which the Santo Sepulcro is fetched by male devotees from the *recamadero* (the keeper of the image) to be 'buried.'

San Fernando, Pampanga: Live Crucifixions

If you're after a more 'savage' display of penitence on Good Friday, San Pedro Cutud is the place to go, where men have themselves actually nailed to a cross after re-enacting the *Via Crucis,* a Kapampangan rendition of the Passion play.

Dozens of hooded men beat their backs raw with bamboo floggers, crawl on dirt roads or bear crosses in the scorching heat. The suffering of the penitents is meant to be intense, and is definitely not for the faint-hearted to witness.

The Good Friday ritual culminates with a procession that begins and ends at the Assumption Cathedral.

Marinduque: Moriones

All throughout Holy Week, you'll find men and women wearing colourful tunics and Roman centurion masks parading on the streets of Boac, Gasan, Santa Cruz, Buenavista and Mogpog in Marinduque.

These masked penitents are called the Moriones (or 'Maryonon') and they're re-enacting the story of Longinus, a half-blind centurion who, according to legend, upon piercing Christ's left side to check if he was dead, had his eyesight fully restored when some of the blood squirted into his eye. This miracle prompted Longinus to convert to Christianity. Unfortunately for Longinus, he was eventually caught and beheaded by his fellow centurions when they found out about his conversion.

Manila: Visita Iglesia

Those who choose not to brave the traffic jams on roads leading out of Manila have their own ways of observing Holy Week. The *Visita Iglesia* ('church visit'), done on Maundy Thursday, is a ritual of visiting seven churches on a single evening. Why seven? The roots of this tradition come from an early Christian practice of visiting the seven great basilicas of Rome. Manila has a long list of old churches dating back to the Spanish regime, and are now considered as cultural heritage sites.

Remembrance of Holy Weeks Past

Senaculo

The *senaculo* is the re-enactment of Christ's life, suffering, death and resurrection, performed by local actors on stage every night from Palm Sunday to Easter Sunday.

I was 15 years old in 1955 when I first watched the senaculo in our hometown. For nine nights, young and old folks alike ventured outdoors to watch the three-hour show.

As a country activity, the senaculo depends for its life on volunteers (actors, director, stage and production crew) and sponsors (for the cost of lights, sound system, costumes, props and sets and, of course, food). There is always a huge welcome and response from the locals. For my town, watching the senaculo players and crew from Morong, Rizal (one of the most popular groups at the time) was a wonderful community activity.

Salubong

As a twelve-year-old, 61 years ago, I had the honour and privilege to be chosen as the angel to lift the *lambong* ('veil of mourning') from the head of Mother Mary, to reveal her happiness at seeing her resurrected son.

The celebration of the *salubong* is an age-old Easter tradition that's unique to the Philippines. Salubong refers to the act of meeting someone who has just arrived. It is a re-enactment of the meeting between Christ and his mother, Mary.

The celebration starts at dawn just before sunrise, with two different processions starting at different points. The first one consists of the icon of the risen Christ carried by men, and the second consists of the statue of Blessed Virgin Mary (covered with a black veil to denote her mourning) carried by women.

The two groups meet at the centre of the churchyard where the two statues are made to face each other under a canopy. The ceremony of the meeting begins with the children's choir singing as Mary approaches Jesus. Under the canopy, an angel lifts the black veil from Our Lady's head, as the crowds cheer. The choir hail the Risen Christ with more hallelujahs. The Dawn Mass is said, and thus begin various activities to celebrate Christ's return.

14. WE ARE A FIESTA-LOVING PEOPLE

There's always a fiesta or festival happening somewhere in the Philippines. Almost every day of the year, in the countless barangays, 1,500 towns, 115 cities and 79 provinces in its 7,100 colourful islands, festive celebrations are being held.

The best fiestas, however, are the summer ones. With school being out through most of April and May, the relaxed atmosphere leads to more vibrant celebrations. The weather is brighter and warmer even if the first rains have arrived. This is the time when nature goes berserk, ripening fruit and grain, hinting of prosperity and therefore giving us a great reason to celebrate.

Not so long ago, a senator suggested that Philippine fiestas be banned, because of the financial burdens they allegedly placed on poor Filipinos who felt obliged to spend money that would be better used on essentials. But this move to eradicate something so deeply rooted was doomed from the beginning. Even in pre-colonial times, our ancestors paid tribute to divine spirits to ask for special favours and good harvests, and rites of passage were marked with elaborate community feasts.

Fiestas are not just an outlet for the gregarious Filipino spirit, but are also a manifestation of our growing national identity and pride of place. What would Lucban be without the Pahiyas, Obando without the fertility dance, Quiapo without the Black Nazarene and Kalibo without the *Ati-atihan*? The fiesta is also a time when people work together to give the community a facelift, when hospitality and friendship are expressed, and even the poorest families can indulge in special delicacies, enjoy a dance and take pleasure in live shows to break the monotony of daily living.

Former President Gloria Macapagal-Arroyo argued for the validity of fiestas in this manner:

'Fiestas are not impediments to, but engines of economic development. They are forums for information dissemination, market transaction and tourism promotion.'

Fiestas can also be harnessed for economic growth. New secular festivals are cropping up all over the country, celebrating crops, livelihoods, sports, legends and arts, and boosting tourists' interest in what used to be little-known places and cultures. This in turn generates income for the locals and the government.

Wherever they go, Filipinos take with them their love for fiestas. Here in Ireland, the Ati-Atihan has graced St. Patrick's Day parades and many a local celebration. In Dublin, not only do we have a fiesta of the Santo Niño ('Holy Child'), we also have a first-Friday novena and a procession on the day of the fiesta itself. Whatever county they are based, Filipinos show off the great variety of Filipino dishes at all their fiesta gatherings.

History of Fiestas

The fiesta as we know it was brought to the Philippines by Spanish priests in the 16th century as a tool for religious conversion, to draw a scattered population 'under the church bells'. Prayer, procession and the ensuing feast brought folks together. But the urge to appease the gods dates back to when our ancestors worshipped natural deities. Thus the Philippine fiesta features a mixture of Christian and folk elements.

In his definitive book *Fiesta* published in 1980, Filipino author Alejandro Roces says:

'It is at once spiritual and sensual, pious and pagan. An eternal moment when the present is collectively experienced now, with the past brought to bear now, and future expectations entertained now.'

There are hundreds of fiestas in the Philippines, and the following are just a few of my favourites.

Santo Niño de Cebu Festival (Third Sunday of January)

The Santo Niño de Cebú (*Balaang Bata sa Sugbo* in Cebuano) is a historic statue of the infant Jesus, venerated by Filipino Catholics for its alleged miraculous qualities. The statue is the oldest surviving Christian image in the country, having been brought in 1521 by Portuguese explorer Ferdinand Magellan as a baptismal gift to Lady Humamay, the chief consort of Rajah Humabon. The image was handed to Lady Humamay by Antonio Pigafetta, along with a statue of the Virgin Mary and a bust of the Ecce Homo.

The statue, approximately 12 inches tall, is believed to be originally made in Flanders, Belgium. It is clothed in expensive fabrics, and bears a gold crown and a variety of scepters mostly donated by devotees. The Santo Niño de Cebu has had such an impact on Filipino Catholic faith that it merited a papal recognition in 1965 from Pope Paul VI.

The Santo Niño image is replicated in many homes and business establishments, with different titles reinterpreted in various areas of the country. The original image is permanently encased within bulletproof glass in a chapel at the Basílica Menor del Santo Niño.

The fiesta of the Holy Child is celebrated every third Sunday of January. There are plenty of places in the Philippines that celebrate this fiesta, but the grandest festivity is the annual Sinulog Festival. In Cebuano, *sulog,* the root word of *sinulog,* describes the motion of water. This flowing movement is mirrored in the Sinulog dance which characterises the festival.

Tourists, both local and foreign, flock to the city of Cebu to witness this event. Viewers and performers alike crowd the streets, dancing to the sound of trumpets, drums and native gongs. This dance signifies the people's acceptance of the Christian faith and the shedding of their pagan beliefs. While the main celebration is held in Cebu City, there are also smaller festivities in the surrounding provinces. While not as grand as the main event, the mini-festivities are just as impressive.

Ati-Atihan Festival (January)

Another colourful festival in honour of the Santo Niño is the Ati-Atihan. Held in Kalibo, Aklan, the Ati-Atihan is considered the wildest among Philippine fiestas and the mother of all Philippine festivals. Its sheer liveliness and boisterousness has made it the most popular choice among OFWs for showcasing Philippine tradition abroad. Celebrants paint their faces with black soot and wear outlandish costumes as they dance in revelry during the last three days of this two-week-long festival. Catholics and non-Catholics alike observe this special day with processions, parades, dancing and merrymaking.

Celebrated in January, the festival peaks on the last three days and ends on the third Sunday of the month. However, people start

106

dancing on the streets as soon as they get over their New Year's Day hangover. The moment they step on the tarmac of Kalibo Airport, tourists are welcomed by the distinct beating of drums in the distance. The entire town centre erupts in frenzied, impromptu dancing, and shouting *'Hala bira! Puwera pasma!'* to the beat of snare drums, bass drums, trumpets, xylophones and a cacophony of other instruments seemingly playing from every corner of Kalibo.

Pahiyas Festival (May)

The name 'Pahiyas' was derived from *payas* which means 'decorations' or 'to decorate' in the Lucban vernacular. Pahiyas, listed by the Department of Tourism as one of the most colourful attractions in the Philippines, aims to honour San Isidro (Saint Isidore), the patron saint of farmers. The preparation occurs weeks before the festival when the locals engage in a friendly competition as they decorate their houses with bright, eye-popping kiping accentuated with farm produce such as rice, plants, vegetables and fruits in varying shapes and sizes.

But it's always the extraordinary kiping that steals the show. These rice wafers are dyed in vibrant colours and moulded to resemble leaves, then woven into lanterns of different shapes and colours. The result is a spectacular sight to behold.

Kiping involves the process of making rice dough or *galapong*. Rice dough is usually prepared by mixing together rice flour with hot water. Because rice does not contain gluten, kneading the dough with cold water or oil results in a dough that will crumble when rolled out. However, adding the rice flour to hot water results in softer and pliable dough that sets and dries quickly once it has been shaped.

Flores de Mayo and Santacruzan (May)

Flores de Mayo ('Flowers of May') and Santacruzan ('Day of the Holy Cross') are both Marian festivals. Flores de Mayo is a floral offering to the Virgin Mary. Every afternoon at five, for the entire month of May, little girls—some dressed up as angels, others as first communicants, glide down to the altar, baskets of flowers in hand, and shower the Virgin with blooms. Amid the shower of petals, the choir sings Marian songs while the elders recite the rosary.

Santacruzan or Day of the Holy Cross is an elaboration of Flores de Mayo. The evening procession re-enacts St. Helena's triumphant search for the True Cross. The town's prettiest maids are dressed to represent female figures from Biblical stories, such as Ruth, Judith, Esther, as well as the various honourific titles attributed to the Virgin Mary. The fairest of the fair plays the coveted role of *Reina* Elena or St. Helena. Garbed in resplendent clothes and crowned with tiaras, the young women and their escorts, accompanied by a brass band and the candle-bearing faithful, walk through the town's main streets, ending at the church in prayer and celebration.

108

Carabao Festival (14–15 May)

On any other day, the carabao or water buffalo is a beast of burden, but every 14th and 15th of May in Pulilan, Bulacan, it becomes king. It is bathed, shaved and brushed, decked with flowers and ribbons and trotted out to town. The Carabao Festival is a tribute to San Isidro (Saint Isidore), the patron saint of labourers.

There are as many carabaos as there are rice farmers at the fiesta. Riding unsaddled, the farmers lead the large animals on their march to church, while being hailed by townfolk waving at them with the year's harvest. On reaching the church, the carabaos are made to genuflect en masse as they receive the priest's blessing for another year of good health and hard work. Not every carabao knows how to bend its knees, or when to bend them, but in Pulilan, farmers have taught their carabaos to do it well.

Sayaw sa Obando or Dance in Obando (15–17 May)

For three consecutive days in mid-May, the normally conservative people of Obando throw caution to the wind to take part in a fertility ritual. Devotees dance to the beat of the fandango as they join a procession meant to invoke the saints for a love object: San Pascual de Baylon for a wife, Santa Clara de Assisi for a husband,

109

and the Virgen de Salambao for a child. Carriages containing images of the three intercessors are the objects of the devotees' ardour. Many reach out to kiss and touch the images as they go past, a few even fall into a swoon. People watching the procession sing out bawdy versions of Santa Clara's song to lend humour to the occasion:

'Santa Clarang pinong-pino
Ang pangako ko ay ganito
Pagdating ko sa Obando
Sasayaw ako ng pandanggo.'

('Delicate Santa Clara
This is my promise
When I arrive in Obando
I shall dance the fandango.')

The procession ends at the altar with more dancing, and even the priests, acolytes and tourists, join the euphoric dancing, making the church resemble a disco.

This peculiar ritual of intercessions is what makes the Obando fiesta unique. Many historians suspect that it is a Christianised version of an older fertility rite, hence the fervent dancing and singing.

15. PARTYING WITH THE DEAD

On the first day of November, Filipinos troop to cemeteries to spend the day in remembrance of their departed loved ones. The celebration of All Saints' Day or the Day of the Dead is one gigantic fiesta—the third most important holiday after Christmas and Lent in the Philippines—and is in stark contrast to the way it is observed in Ireland. The universal aspect of Catholicism falls short when it comes to remembering the dead. But for a regular Mass on the first of November and a run-of-the-mill Cemetery Day in July or August, All Saints' Day is practically a non-event here in Ireland, and the unpredictable Irish weather certainly doesn't help!

Though the subject matter may be considered morbid from the perspective of some other cultures, Filipinos approach the Day of the Dead joyfully. Even if it occurs roughly at the same time as Halloween, the traditional mood is much brighter and emphasises honouring the lives of the deceased and celebrating the continuation of life.

Death rituals are important in all cultures and have one

111

objective: to bring together relatives and friends for a communal coping with grief and anxiety. The rituals vary with each culture, reflecting differences in social circumstances. Western death rituals, as in Ireland, are usually very solemn, mainly allowing expressions of grief through ceremonies that are simple, private and brief. In contrast, many cultures, including our own, have much more elaborate and prolonged death rituals, allowing as many people as possible to participate. They are noisy affairs, almost rude and blasphemous to the outsider, and include drinking and gambling during the wake.

I remember the shock on my husband's face the first time he went to a wake in the Philippines. In the church where the wake was held, he saw people playing mah-jong and engaging in banter. It took him as much time to understand the Filipinos' peculiar approach to death as it did me to get over the brevity of Irish wakes.

Observing death rituals gives us insights into culture. Filipinos deal with trouble by joking, almost as if to trivialise a misfortune. With death, we become celebratory, literally calling on friends to eat, drink and be merry. It's a chance for different people to celebrate and pay tribute to their relationship with the deceased.

Like most Christian festivals, All Saints' Day had its origins in pagan rituals. The ancient Gaels believed that the time of the year between 31 October and 1 November, known as the Celtic New Year, was when the boundaries between the dead and the living disappeared. The Church under Popes Gregory III and IV decided to neutralise this pagan ritual by holding All Saints' Day on 1 November. Initially, the time was a period of fasting as well as the holding of vigils. What began as a time of remembrance of the Christian martyrs evolved into the present custom of remembering all the dead.

Filipino Christians strongly believe that death is not the end, but just the beginning of a new stage in life. We see the Day of the Dead as an 'opportunity to be with' our departed loved ones. Tombs are cleaned or repainted, candles lit, flowers offered and Masses celebrated. Families usually camp in cemeteries, with many spending a night or two by their relatives' tombs. Card games, eating, drinking, singing and dancing are common activities during the day.

My husband has now retired, but while working in Dublin, he earned the reputation among officemates as 'the man who likes funerals.' It came about because the few times he went home to his hometown in Limerick to bury old friends, he would always say once he got back, 'It was a great funeral!'

It might be strange to his fellow Irish, but I reckon this is just his way of showing how he has adopted the Filipino way of celebrating the dead.

16. GLOBAL FILIPINOS, GLOBAL CHRISTMAS

One of the anomalies of western music when it's listened to in tropical countries is that you end up, for instance, with Filipinos 'dreaming of a white Christmas.' As soon as the '-ber' months arrive, streets in the Philippines resound with Irving Berlin's classic song, igniting shopping centres with their extravagant display of goods to win the race for profit.

The Filipino Christmas is rooted in religion and faith, but growing materialism and commercialism have crept in, luring the public to buy, buy, buy!

How did our once highly spiritualised country become westernised in the way we celebrate Christmas?

The first Nativity Mass in the Philippines was held in the early 14th century by an Italian Franciscan friar named Oderic de Perdenonen. The *Encyclopedia of the Philippines,* a 1936 publication edited by by Zoilo M. Galang and Camilo Osias, mentions that Odoric and his compatriots were not missionaries but refugees from religious persecutions in Europe. On his way back to Europe, Odoric landed on Christmas day on the shoreline of what is now Pangasinan. The priest decided to convert the handful of natives who met his party. After planting a black cross on the ground, Odoric held a Natale Mass for the new converts.

On 16 March 1521, Ferdinand Magellan landed on the island of Cebu and claimed the 'new' country for Spain. It was later named 'Philippines' in honour of the Spanish monarch, Philip II. The seeds of Christianity were planted throughout the archipelago by zealous Spanish missionaries. It was they who instilled in our ancestors the love for Christmas, the devotion to the Santo Niño, and the spirit of Christian generosity and gratitude.

But long before the era of Spanish colonisation and Christianisation, the natives were already making thanksgiving offerings to their gods before venturing out to labour in their fields in the early mornings. This practice was to be the key to one of the Filipinos' most treasured Christmas traditions.

Dawn Masses

As Christmas coincides with harvest time, a Spanish friar cleverly scheduled a mass at dawn, knowing that converted farmers would easily relate to worship before work. This was also inspired by the outdoor morning Masses which Fray Diego de Soria started in

Mexico in 1587.

These dawn Masses, aptly called *Misa de Gallo* ('Mass of the rooster') but more popularly known as *simbang gabi* ('evening worship'), commence on 16 December—the official start of the Christmas period in the Philippines—and are held for nine consecutive mornings, just as in a novena.

Devotees rise before daybreak and brave the dark and the morning chill brought about by northeastern monsoon winds. In some places, brass bands briskly parade down the streets, playing popular marches and lively dance music to energise those who are still struggling to wake up. These brass bands are the 'alarm clocks' of Christmas—breaking the early-morning silence to announce that the dawn everyone has been waiting for has finally arrived.

Eastern and Western Influences

Many beautiful European traditions have greatly influenced the observance of Philippine Christmas over the years—we too have Santa Claus or St Nicholas, Christmas trees, mistletoe, carols, yuletide candles and Christmas cards.

During the Hispanic era, several Mexican yuletide traditions crossed the seas to the Philippines. With the American invasion in 1898, the Thomasites introduced some American Christmas rituals to locals. All these have somehow found their place in the mix of merriment and piety that is Filipino Christmas today.

We have the *belen* (crèche), the *parol* (lantern) and the dawn masses as evidence of our Hispanic past. The American Santa Claus is a ubiquitous character in shopping centres, a source of delight and terror for little kids. Christmas trees, real or not, are embellished the American way. We hang wreaths, roast chestnuts, kiss under the mistletoe, exchange cards and presents, and sing 'Auld Lang Syne'— all western traditions.

Neighbouring countries such as China, Japan, Malaysia, Indonesia and India have also left their distinctive marks on how we observe Christmas—the elaborate dishes prepared on Christmas Eve, ethnic dances, fluvial parades and noisy firecrackers.

Paskong Pinoy ('Filipino Christmas') effortlessly melds the new with the old, the unfamiliar with the familiar, as well as Christian beliefs with tribal customs, local myths and superstitions.

The Balikbayan

The Christmas season also ushers in the homecoming of overseas Filipinos—the *balikbayan*—filling jumbo jets and congesting the airport with emotional arrivals and cartloads of presents. Husbands, wives, sons, daughters, sisters, brothers, aunts and uncles from all over the world rush home to enjoy Christmas.

Those who cannot return home simply take Pasko with them, transplanting Filipino customs wherever they may be.

Global Filipinos celebrate a global Christmas, no matter which part of the world they are.

17. THE WAY WE ARE: OUR STRENGTHS AND WEAKNESSES

What Is Culture?

Whenever he writes about Filipino culture, Fr Gorospe starts with this disclaimer:

> 'When we speak of traditions and values, we do not claim they are peculiar or exclusive to any one country. Although values or traditions may manifest themselves differently or uniquely in the Philippines, they are universal values.'

Culture is defined as the common learned way of life of a society, which is reflected in its customs, traditions, folkways, mores and beliefs, as well as in the totality of tools, techniques, artifacts, etc., that are used and practised by the people in that society. Values, attitudes and norms are also part of culture. Values are the things that people consider to be good, important and desirable in life.

Filipinos have a reputation for being cultural hybrids. The population of the Philippines reflects the great variety of external

119

influences which have blended with our original Malay culture: Arabian, Chinese, Indo-Chinese, Hindu-Indonesian, Spanish-Catholic and American-Protestant.

However, the cultural matrix of the modern Filipino already existed long before the Spanish colonisers arrived. Our cultural traits were borrowed from a wide variety of other cultures, but combined in such a way that the result is distinctly Filipino.

Throughout our country's history as a colony, Filipinos have mounted significant rebellions, whilst at the same adapting remarkably to the invaders. This adaptability and resilient flexibility were probably a survival mechanism and our ancestors' pliancy before colonisers, a useful strategy.

In allowing new forms of life to take root and grow, Philippine culture has not been overgrown. Which parts of culture have continued? In the essay 'Is There a Real Philippine Culture?' in the book *All Things to All Men* (1988), Miriam Adeney explains:

> 'Bilateral kinship structures, respect for elders including elder brothers and sisters, many opportunities for women, respect for the dead, values like *pakikisama, utang na loob, pakikipagkapwa.* These appear era after era.'

Values: What Makes Up the Filipino Character?

In 1992, the Philippine Senate, headed by Senator Leticia Shahani, sponsored a study called 'Filipino Value and Moral Development'. The study was conducted by a task force headed by Dr. Patricia Licuanan. The findings were based on bibliographic surveys, interviews and consultations with researchers and practitioners in the behavioural and social sciences, education and social welfare, journalists and social analysts; a nationwide survey of 2000 respondents; and focus group discussions among residents of an urban poor resettlement area in Bagong Bayan, Dasmariñas, Cavite. The result was a report called 'A Moral Recovery Program: Building a People, Building a Nation'. The report discussed, among other things, the strengths and weaknesses of Filipinos as a people. The following is a list of those findings.

Strengths of the Filipino Character

Ability and will to survive

Filipinos are born survivors, a trait manifested in our capacity for endurance despite difficult times, and our ability to get by on very little. Filipinos make do with what is available in the environment. This survival instinct is related to the Filipinos' other strengths--a basic optimism, flexibility and adaptability, hard work and a deep

121

faith in God.

Faith and religiosity

Filipinos have a deep faith in God. Our innate religiosity enables us to comprehend and genuinely accept reality in the context of God's will. Thus, many people tend to take tragedy and misfortune as part of life, and even the poorest are still optimistic.

Hard work and industriousness

Filipinos are industrious workers. There's an innate desire in us to be able to afford a decent life for our family and raise our standard of living. When given the right opportunities and incentives, we will pour all our energy into our work.

Flexibility, adaptability and creativity

Filipinos can adjust and adapt to changes in their circumstances and surrounding environment, both physical and social. Unplanned and anticipated events are never overly disturbing or disorienting, as our flexible nature helps us take these changes in stride.

Joy and humour

Filipinos have a cheerful and fun-loving approach to life and its ups and downs. We have a pleasant disposition, a wacky sense of humour and a propensity for finding joy in trivial things, all of which contribute not only to our charm but also to the indomitability of the Filipino spirit.

Family orientation

Filipinos possess a genuine and deep love for family. To us, 'family' doesn't just refer to the nuclear one—it includes all our relatives, even those not related to us by blood. To us, our family is the source of personal identity, and emotional and material support, and our main commitment and responsibility.

Pakikipagkapwa-tao

Filipinos are an empathetic people. We regard others with dignity and respect, and deal with them as fellow human beings. Relationships (*pakikipagkapwa*) are very important to us. Perhaps this is because most of us have spent most of our lives intimately within a group, and learned early on that the world doesn't revolve around us. We see in our daily interactions how intertwined people's lives are.

The importance that Filipinos attach to pakikipagkapwa is clearly reflected in our values system. Utang na loob (debt of gratitude), *pakikisama* (smooth personal relationship), personalism and intrusion are ramifications of the central value of pakikipagkapwa and are therefore better understood in the light of that value.

Hiya

Hiya has been widely translated as 'shame'. Understood in this context, *hiya* as a cultural trait gives the impression of a group of people who are extremely other-directed, lacking in character and backbone. However, when seen in the context of its more frequent usage, what you'll see is a people who are moved more by concern for others' welfare than by fear of group censure.

Let us take the case of a person who invites a friend to visit an elderly neighbour at two o'clock in the afternoon. The friend replies, 'Not this time. *Nakakahiya naman kay Manong. Nag-sisiesta iyon dapat sa oras na ito.'* ('It is embarrassing. He should be taking a nap at this time of the day.) Obviously, the person feels hiya out of a strong sense of propriety. True *pakikipagkapwa* demands that a Filipino be moved by *hiya* and not cause inconvenience to other people.

Pakikisama or smooth personal relationship

This trait is closely related to utang na loob and stems from being part of a group. As members of a group, we are expected to value loyalty and sensitivity to other people's feelings, and to work together based on the concept of 'give and take'. *Pakikisama* is all about maintaining good public relations and avoiding conflict with the leader or the majority of a group. This is closely linked with *hiya* which controls to a large extent the behaviour of the individual and is likely dependent on what others will think, say and do. Because of *hiya*, Filipinos sometimes find it hard to say no, especially when the request comes from a respected person or the group that they belong to.

Amor propio

Amor propio translates to 'self-love' or, as a Filipino trait, 'self-esteem'. Our amor propio is responsible for our refusal to beg for favours, or even to agree to a lucrative proposition straight away, no matter how much we want to.

Utang na loob

Utang na loob is at the heart of many Filipino relationships. Whenever someone does you a favour, you are expected to pay that person back in one way or another.

A cultural example would be the practice of *bolhon* ('cooperation') in the Visayas. Farmers work together to till the land, with the group working on each other's plots in succession. The plot owner acts as the boss when their land is being tilled. This way, each farmer gets a turn as the boss and as a worker.

Another example is the custom of *abuloy* ('contribution') which is given to the family of a person who has just died. The members of the family note the people who gave them abuloy, and remember to do the same for their families.

Showing your utang na loob to someone who's done you a good deed can take many forms, from rendering professional services for free, helping them or their relatives get a job or paying for the tuition fee of a friend's child.

Personalism

Personalism, or the quality of being personal, is something that Filipinos value. Being personal with each other guarantees intimacy, warmth, and security of kinship and friendship in getting things done. This value can be the foundation of genuine commitment and deep loyalty.

In the Philippines, a personal touch is required if you want to get things done. Filipinos are more likely to respond positively to leaders who are charismatic, or at least take the time to communicate with them in person.

Weaknesses of the Filipino Character

Extreme personalism

Why do some Filipino organisations fail? Most of the time, it's due to a lack of trust between contracting parties if the *kilala* ('personal reference') system has not been tapped. There is short-lived enthusiasm for supporting and maintaining groups outside of families and circles of friends. This belief that everything is better when it's personal can be damaging in many ways.

We tend to be uncomfortable with bureaucracy, with rules and regulations, and standard procedures, all of which tend to be impersonal. We tend to ignore them or we ask for exemptions. Personal contacts are involved in any transaction and these are difficult to turn down. Preference is usually given to family and friends in hiring, delivery of services and even in voting. Extreme personalism thus leads to graft and corruption, a problem that has hounded Philippine society for a really long time.

The *kanya-kanya* syndrome

Filipinos tend to have a self-serving attitude that generates a

126

feeling of envy and competitiveness toward others, particularly one's peers who seem to have gained some status or prestige. The *kanya-kanya* syndrome is also evident in the personal ambition and the drive for power and status that is completely insensitive to the common good. Personal and in-group interests reign supreme.

This characteristic is also evident in the lack of a sense of service among people in government offices. Many civil servants behave as if doing their jobs was an extra perk that the public have to pay for. The kanya-kanya system dampens the community spirit and tramples people's rights.

Extreme family-centredness

Some Filipinos' excessive loyalty to their family ends up being detrimental to the community. This is most evident in politics where many people in power use their office to promote their families' own interests. Political dynasties, factionalism and patronage politics are the products of family-centredness among Filipinos.

Lack of discipline

As a people, Filipinos are notoriously relaxed towards time and quality. This lack of discipline manifests in poor time management (hence, the hard-to-live-down 'Filipino time') and procrastination, and an aversion to strict procedures, which results in lack of standardisation and poor quality control.

We tend to be impatient and unable to delay gratification. We'd rather find a shortcut or skirt the rules (the *'palusot'* syndrome), and

127

this often leads to trouble. We are guilty of *ningas cogon*, starting projects with full vigour and interest but once these fade, we just leave the projects unfinished. Our lack of discipline often results in rule violations that lead to more serious transgressions, and a lax work ethic characterised by carelessness and absence of follow-through.

Passivity and lack of initiative

Filipinos are generally passive and lack initiative. We rely on our leaders and the government to tell us what to do, and many of us tend to swallow everything that figures of authority tell us, no matter how questionable it is.

Our complacency means that we rarely approach a problem with any sense of urgency. We also have a high tolerance for inefficiency, poor service and even violations of our basic rights. In many ways, it can be said that the Filipino is too patient and accepting of suffering (*matiisin*). Too easily resigned to their fate, Filipinos are thus easily oppressed and exploited.

Colonial mentality

The Philippines has been an independent country for more than 50 years, but sadly, colonial mentality lives on. It manifests itself in two ways: first, in the lack of patriotism and active awareness, appreciation for, and love of the Philippines; second, in our actual preference for foreign, specifically western, things.

Our openness to outside influences and willingness to adopt

new ideas and cultures have made it difficult for us to have a deep core of Philippine history and language. The result is a cultural vagueness or weakness that makes Filipinos extraordinarily susceptible to the wholesale acceptance of modern mass culture, which is often western. Thus, many of us have this (usually false) belief that anything foreign—from fashion, entertainment to technology, lifestyles and even physical appearance—is better than what Filipinos have.

PART THREE

DISCOVER IRELAND

'Diversity is the magic. It is the first manifestation, the first beginning of the differentiation of a thing and of simple identity. The greater the diversity, the greater the perfection.'

—**Thomas Berry**

18. PLANTING SPUDS IS ALWAYS FUN!

When we moved to Ireland from the Philippines in 1977, my husband Jim thought he could augment his income by growing potatoes, just as his father did. He grew up on a farm in Limerick but was a journalist by profession. 'I didn't know my ass from my elbow,' he admitted, 'but it seemed so simple to grow potatoes for a start.'

He rented a plot from the Dublin Corporation, and agreed to share the work and produce with his friend Jack. Jack, bearer of a rural, spud-digging pedigree from Cappatagal in County Galway, had also just returned from abroad after marrying a Filipina. He too wanted to grow and eat his own food.

In April, the two of them surveyed their allotment, which measured a tenth of an acre. The ground was covered in withered hay, some as tall as two feet. They decided to burn the hay and dig the plots with spades just like their fathers did. Digging would be good, they reckoned. Then they went for a pint.

They figured that 'scutch' grass was the culprit. After consulting a dictionary, they found out that it was actually called couch grass.

132

They would have to plough the plot to get rid of the weed.

A tractor rented for £10 did the job but left the land deeply trenched that the two lads had no idea what to do next. The sods were huge and craggy. They kicked these around, prodded them with spades, and decided to work out the problem over a pint.

Jim and Jack couldn't agree on what to do next, apart from having to stir the ploughed earth somehow. Putting their heads together hadn't really gotten them anywhere apart from Courtney's pub.

Finally, Jim let Jack have his way and, with a lot of grunting and puffing, he coaxed every two lines of upturned sod into a sort of drill, leaving the matted couch untouched at the bottom. He dug in the seed potatoes every 18 inches or so, each one lovingly cushioned on a fistful of hops.

The stalks came up and so did the couch grass. I had to come out and help get rid of the weed. In July and August, on our knees, we tried to keep the couch at bay, or at least stop it from dwarfing the stalks. It seemed to grow as fast as we pulled it.

Harvest time came at the end of August and our first batch of Record potatoes was a welcome sight on our table. I watched Jim stuff himself so that not even a single small one would go in the bin. They were after all the first spuds he ever grew. The spud-growing link between the Kennedy generation was being preserved, unbroken.

Then one mid-October evening, he found a letter from the

Corporation waiting for him when he got home from work.

> 'Dear Mr. K,
> I refer to your letting of allotment No. X. Although you have paid for this plot for the coming season, it seems that it has not been worked. As there are a number of people in the waiting list I will have to allocate this plot to one of these unless I hear from you by return.
>
> Yours, etc.'

Jim swore by the *mailins* and *scilleans* of his ancestors. It was evident that some agent of the Corporation had inspected his plot and couldn't distinguish between potato stalks and couch grass in the distance.

To add the final nail to the coffin, I just had to tell him I had seen potatoes selling at 95p a sack in the local supermarket. Then I began totting up what he had spent on allotment fees, seed potatoes, ploughing, hops, fertiliser and a new handle for the spade.

'Yours cost us £3.80 a sack, not counting labour.'

'A trifle expensive,' he admitted, knowing in his heart that if I added the price of the pints he and Jack had drunk, they would be very expensive potatoes, indeed!

Some Irishmen are not a patch on their fathers.

19. SUNNY SPELLS AND SCATTERED SHOWERS

Believe it or not, I am fascinated by the Irish weather. I love it for two reasons: first, I dislike the extreme heat in the Philippines so much that the coolness of the Irish air is actually a relief for me, and second, the Irish weather is a great conversational piece. If I want to break the ice in any gathering or even when seated on the bus next to an Irish person, I just need to comment on the weather, and a spirited conversation starts straight away.

I discovered that the Irish take their weather seriously. Instead of the usual, 'How are you?' their daily greetings to one another are exclamations about the weather: 'Thank God for a fine day,' 'Lovely day,' 'Grand day,' 'Soft day,' 'Watery sun' or 'Horrible day!' Sometimes the greetings are punctuated with questions: 'Will it rain?', 'Will the rain ever stop?' or 'Will the sun shine today?'

The Irish are obsessed with the weather in a way that we

Filipinos are not. The tropical climate in the Philippines is basically simple and predictable. It's normally dry from November to June and wet from July to October—that's it. The only time we pay attention to the weather forecast is when the typhoon season comes.

Irish weather, on the other hand, is very fickle. Not only does it have four seasons but it's not uncommon for the Irish to experience the climatic variations of all four seasons on a single day. Even in the summer, you have to be prepared just in case it rains or the temperature drops considerably.

The secret to coping with the Irish weather lies in taking the correct clothing. Always prepare for moderately mild weather, and make sure that you supplement your outfit with a warm jumper or a rainproof top. A hat is a good accessory; an umbrella, probably not.

Be careful on sunny days especially on the beach, as the breeze can cool you while the sun still burns your skin. And take sensible footwear. I remember how a group of newly arrived Filipino nurses was so excited with the snow that they galloped about in their *tsinelas* ('slippers'), only to suffer from blisters later. Take note also that most rural, and even some urban, areas are best described as 'rugged terrain' and the ground is bound to be wet occasionally.

While it is true that there are no major temperature differences between the seasons and that rain is likely every other day, the Irish weather is manageable.

Temperatures will rarely go below 0°C and only occasionally

goes higher than 20°C, with June, July and August being the warmest months, and January and February the coldest. However, freezing spells tend to bring the country to a grinding halt and even a sprinkling of snow will have most drivers panicking.

'Never mind the weather,' my now grown-up children advise, 'we have to do what we have to do.' Indeed, come hail, rain or shine, nothing can discourage them from going out to have fun or attend work-related meetings. The Irish weather has hardened them.

Extremes are not unknown in Ireland. The summer of 2006 was the hottest on record for ages, but 2013 and 2014 set the record for a real Irish heat wave, with temperatures going up as high as 30°C!

Unsurprisingly, the Irish have plenty of weather-related clichés. In a 21 June 2014 *Irish Times* article, Shane Hegarty compiled a handy list of failsafe news topics about heat waves, including these gems:

- 'Something, something, something, "since records began".'
- Animals and plants being confused by the weather.
- Sales of all or any of the following: ice cream, barbecues, fans and cider. And a line about a fight breaking at a B&Q shop over the last paddling pool in stock.
- A journalist trying to fry an egg on the hood of car or on the pavement, and failing.
- Farmers welcoming the warm weather.
- Farmers becoming concerned with the hot weather.
- Farmers saying that any more hot weather will be a disaster to the rural economy.

- Enjoy the weather while you can. Rain will be returning next week.

- Every report on the weather obsessed with how long this is going to last.

- Is this a result of global warming?

- How did MET Eireann get it so wrong?

Irish weather could drive an unsuspecting newcomer a bit mad, but living for a long time in the country helps you get used to it. Just take this conversation, as told by the Indian Jesuit priest and psychotherapist Anthony de Mello, between a traveller and a shepherd:

> **Traveller:** 'What kind of weather are we going to have today?'
> **Shepherd:** 'The kind of weather I like.'
> **Traveller:** 'How do you know it will be the kind of weather you like?'
> **Shepherd:** 'Having found out, sir, that I cannot always get what I like, I have learnt always to like what I get. So I am quite sure we will have the kind of weather I like.'

20. GASTRONOMIC INITIATIONS

'Go on, try it.'

Their cousins were prodding my two teenagers, Patrick, 15, and Noriana, 14, to eat *balut*, a popular delicacy in the Philippines. We had just arrived for a one-month holiday in June 1998, the first time for my children, and our relatives were eager to initiate them into Filipino cuisine.

'What is it, really?' Patrick wasn't sure whether it was a duck or chicken egg. Noriana was examining it, holding one of the warm eggs against the light trying to see what was inside. A dozen balut were in front of them, freshly bought from a street vendor that evening.

'Why is it black?' Nan queried. One cousin, quick on the draw, cracked a balut open, and a cooked fertilised embryo with discernible feathers came into full view! He drank the 'soup' with gusto and with relish chewed and ate the whole lot in one gulp.

That did the trick. My two children followed suit, and were soon competing with their cousins on how many balut they could finish in one seating!

It must be genetic, but my Nan and Patrick took to Filipino food after just a single try, and since then have eaten any Filipino food that's offered them.

My first exposure to Irish food was on the morning after my arrival in Dublin. Waking up from a jet-lagged sleep, I was welcomed at the table by a plate of full Irish breakfast. Also called the 'big fry', every item in this meal has been cooked in a frying pan—bacon, sausage, black and white pudding, egg and tomatoes—and served with homemade brown bread.

Mary Mills, my sister-in-law and future friend who taught me the Irish way of life in my first year of initiation, was at the table, ready with a pot of freshly made tea. She kept refilling my cup with the hot drink. I never thought tea could be so refreshing. I hadn't had it with milk and sugar before, and it tasted very good. Back home, we would drink tea black and only when we had an upset stomach!

Now I drink tea at least three times a day. To me, what makes tea great is the drop of fresh pasteurised milk in it, something that we don't have in ready supply in the Philippines.

I also got to know the Irish staple food—potatoes. I didn't realise that there were so many varieties—Kerr Pink, Queen, Rooster, Golden Wonder, Record, etc. It reminds me of our own varieties of rice—Wagwag, Basmati, Milagrosa, Macan and Miracle, just to name a few.

The Great Famine

My husband's family is from Brackile, Pallasgrean in Co. Limerick. On many of our trips there, we would stay in a thatched house which is more than a hundred years old and was renovated as a holiday home. Across the road is a two-hectare grassland which is a grim reminder of the famine that struck the country in 1845.

'During the height of the famine,' Jim told me, 'our ancestors exchanged that land for a bag of yellow meal which was then the only food available. Our ancestors survived the famine but lost a great piece of land.'

The Great Potato Famine was caused by bad weather that led to a fungal disease called potato blight. Potato blight has a cyclical nature, and there were small-scale famines every few years leading up to the tragic one in 1847. More than a million Irish people died of starvation and diseases as a result of that famine. Another two and a half million were forced to emigrate, changing the economy and social structure of Ireland forever.

What didn't change though was the love for and dependence on spuds (slang for 'potatoes'). Whenever there are Irish guests at a Filipino party, I always find myself reminding the organisers to include potatoes on the menu, just as Irish people who are familiar with Filipino dietary preferences always remember to cook rice for their Filipino guests.

In the 1970s, Asian groceries were a rarity in Ireland, making it nearly impossible for me to cook Filipino dishes. This proved to be a blessing as I soon realised that with a little bit of open-mindedness and goodwill, I could adjust to another way of cooking and eating. While I missed Filipino fruits, vegetables and rice, I was soon enjoying meals cooked from bacon, cabbage, broccoli, carrot, and turnips and, of course, potatoes!

Slainte (Irish toast for 'good health')!

21. MIND YOUR LANGUAGE

When my first baby was born, I was delighted when neighbours, friends and relations came to see my newborn. 'What a gorgeous baby!' exclaimed a neighbour. 'Lovely child,' remarked another. 'He's grand,' declared a friend.

Everyone else who came to visit used similar adjectives to express their admiration for my baby. This left me wondering if I had given birth to another Marilyn Monroe. The only trouble was my baby was a boy.

I realised that Irish English can differ in some ways from my American English and Filipino English. The Irish will not just say 'Thanks'; they'll say 'Thank you very much' or 'Thank you very much, indeed.'

Things are never just okay or nice. They're 'Fantastic!', 'Brilliant', 'Great!', 'Mighty!', 'Legend!' or even 'Massive!' Through the years I have learned how to use these expressions and discovered that they are great for making people feel good.

But it is not only the exclamations and superlatives that I had to learn; there were also Irish phrases unfamiliar to me. 'Isn't it a soft day today?' greeted an Irishman over the road. Seeing my puzzled face, he very kindly explained, 'A soft day is that kind of weather that happens in Ireland. It indicates a degree of raininess where the rain seems to drift around in the air rather than actually fall down.'

When I asked for directions to the post office, I was told that it was 'below in the village.' There's the word 'blow-in', which refers to someone who has moved into an area where they have no roots and are just as likely to go away again or may stay there for good. The family doctor is called the GP (general practitioner), a pharmacist is referred to as a chemist, and 'grind' means private tuition or tutoring.

Craic means a good laugh and can be had without the use of drugs, although alcohol is usually present at most craic-getting sessions. 'Press' refers to the wardrobe or kitchen drawers, and 'good luck' is another way of saying good-bye. No wonder then that Filipino nurses have had to master an entirely different set of medical and hospital terminology in the workplace.

There's one thing that I really love about the Irish—it's the constant saying of the word 'sorry'. It's something unique to Ireland—men, women and children apologising all day. On a crowded bus, people mutter sorry as they squeeze past you. In the shop, the shopkeeper will say the magic word to get your attention, 'Sorry, can I help you?' The mother will accost her child, 'Sorry, darling, you cannot have that.'

And it is so infectious! As you are still wondering if they are indeed apologising, you suddenly hear it coming out of your own mouth: sorry, as your phone is ringing and you are apologising for the noise.

Then there is the phrase 'your man'. This doesn't refer to one's boyfriend, partner or husband. I discovered this when my husband was asking a salesman in a shop about the cost of an appliance, and the salesman couldn't tell. Jim said, 'May I speak to your man?' referring to the shop manager. He would also often ask a friend, 'How's your man doing?' which may refer to the friend's father or some other male relative.

I discovered that language is a significant element of a people's culture. In language is embedded the thought patterns, the world-view and the deepest experiences of a race. Language influences both our relationship with the environment and with other people. For instance, the Filipino language is very much centred on food because it's something that gives us a lot of pleasure.

How are we supposed to understand one another, then, when we do not share a common cultural experience? Living in multicultural clusters within a global village, we all face this question every day. What kind of communication is needed by a pluralistic society to be both culturally diverse and unified in communication goals?

Susan Schneider and Jean-Louis Barsoux, authors of the 2002

book, *Managing Across Cultures,* assert that our language is affected by our environment, specifically the weather:

'The use of language may represent the most visible yet the least understood influence on our world view. It is through language that we formulate thoughts and that we experience the world.'

More clues about culture can be found in formalised exchanges. In today's multicultural Ireland, the importance of these rituals should not be overlooked. Culture is like a code—what is observed must be deciphered; we must search the meaning beneath the activity.

22. NOW I BELONG

I've lived in Ireland for almost four decades now. I feel so Irish that when I walk down the road and mingle with people, I forget the colour of my skin, my accent and the fact that I'm a Filipino.

Don't get me wrong, it's not that I'm no longer a Filipino; this God-given birth right will always be cherished and upheld.

What I'm saying is, I'm very happy in Ireland. I have integrated into this country.

For once I was a stranger, now I'm one of them. Once I was an outsider, now I belong.

The way I see it, integration is that sense of home one acquires through years of mingling, accepting and identifying with a people. It's allowing space in your heart for others to come in and influence you. It's that sense of ownership of the success of the Celtic Tiger period, being thrilled with the triumphs of River Dance and the Lord of the Dance, and cheering with my husband at the triumphs of the Irish in sports such as rugby, soccer, golf, hurling and football. It is being at one with fellow mothers as we walked down the road to take the children to and from school, enjoying a clean-up project, sharing expertise with others in the gardening club, visiting the sick and the elderly, and attending funerals.

It is meeting halfway the culture of my host country. Years ago, when my children were small, a Filipino friend visiting me heard a five-year-old playmate of my children call me 'Vising'. 'Oh, my God,' she protested, 'that girl has no respect!'

I don't blame my friend—we grew up in a country where elders are addressed with honourifics. Here in Ireland, however, it is acceptable to call a person by their first name, regardless of their age or status. This is not disrespect. Enda, the Taoiseach, will always be called by his first name, yet he is respected. I couldn't fault a five-year-old for calling me by my first name. She wasn't being rude; she was just being her Irish self.

The Courage to Be an Immigrant

In a 2010 speech to Irish immigrants in the UK, President Mary MacAleese said:

> 'You need courage to be an emigrant, to be a stranger with a heart-breaking loneliness for home, and a deep human need to be made feel at home in a new homeland.'

Every immigrant experiences some level of heartache. Even a

romantic immigrant like me, with support from a husband and Irish relations, wasn't spared from going through the process of adaptation.

In my case, it was no joke raising children and acculturating at the same time. I was not even juggling a career and family life then, as my husband and I decided that it would be best for me to stay at home. There were few jobs available at that time, and I didn't know enough of the Irish language to complete my teaching qualifications. Fortunately for us, being on a single salary was quite enough to pay the mortgage, take care of our kids, manage the house and pay for a few holidays. However, having worked all my adult life, I felt redundant and unhappy.

One cold winter day made more miserable by lashing rain and the sound of my young children crying, I went to answer the door. A young Irish lady greeted me. 'Good morning,' she said with a smile. 'May I help you?'

Good heavens! I couldn't believe it. Was this an answer to my prayer? Somebody was offering to help me—for free!

I was just so delighted to welcome her and we started talking. I learned that she was a member of a religious organisation, and as a prerequisite for admission, she had to do a one-month 'novitiate' by helping people in our area. She was a volunteer! At that moment, all I wanted was someone to mind the children for a few hours so I could take a nap. But she did more than that—she even cleaned the house and tidied up the garden!

That fateful visit opened my eyes to the reality that there was a big community out there that was willing and ready to help, if I would just ask. I was not alone! I discovered that volunteers in Ireland are such a valuable group of people. Raising my kids became more manageable, thanks to the volunteers who existed in every parish.

From Birth to Death

In every stage of life, from birth to death, there are volunteers and community groups ready to answer your call. For instance, there are mother-and-toddler groups that bring young mothers together for a chat and a chance to relax, while their toddlers play and make new friends. There are the Gaelic Athletics Association (GAA) summer camps, some run by parents, aimed at coaching children in different types of sports.

My children's first trips to France and Germany were facilitated by adult volunteers. A lot of blissful adventures at theme parks, zoos and museums, and enjoying sports such as swimming, bowling and skateboarding would not have been possible for the kids if not for the generosity of dedicated people giving their time and energy to good causes.

If it is in giving that we receive, what better way to respond to this generosity but to give something in return?

'I'm bored!'

You'll often hear this from children who don't know what to do with themselves during the long summer holidays. The trouble is, you cannot simply be concerned with your own children. When trying to think of something to keep your own kids busy, you'll also have to think about what they and their friends can do together.

So what did we do? There were some ten children ranging from ages 7 to 12 in our neighbourhood. One of the girls, the leader of the pack, suggested that we stage a play. Parents and children agreed to do *Cinderella*. The script borrowed from the library was ready, the cast were chosen, times of rehearsals were scheduled and our back garden was chosen as the venue. The kids made their own costumes from all sorts of things. The performance, though not as good as what we may see at the Helix or the Gaiety, delighted the people in the neighbourhood.

This simple activity to keep the kids busy led to a permanent summer project. The Lucan Youth Fun in our parish, organised in the 1980s, continues to this day, benefitting some 600 schoolchildren every summer. And it's completely run by volunteer-parents.

23. BRINGING UP A BABY IN A COLD CLIMATE

Nobody was in sight. I had been looking out of the window of our house for an hour, and had yet to see another human being pass by. It was winter and I had just come out of the hospital with my baby. I was desperate to see someone, never mind talk to them. I presumed people were busy with their own lives in the confines of their own homes.

I felt homesick. I was missing the sight of so many people back home, the sounds of conversations and laughter; dogs barking, shouts of children playing, and peddlers selling their wares. These sounds would be enough to keep you company if you are homebound and alone. Most people in the Philippines would not want to be on their own. There is always a relation, a friend or a neighbour to keep one company, so much so that if someone is seen going somewhere on their own, they'd get asked, 'Where is your companion?'

Of course, there are almost 100 million people in the

Philippines, a far cry from Ireland's population of 4.6 million! In Ireland, it's rare to come across another person on a country road. It can be so frustrating if you're lost and all you need is one person to help you find your way.

On Circumcision

Patrick, my first baby, was born on a freezing day in January.

'When will my baby be circumcised?' I asked a nurse my third day in the hospital. She was taken aback and struggled to reply, but later told me that circumcision isn't practised in Ireland.

My husband thinks that the weather has something to do with it. He gathered there was no need for male circumcision in a cold climate. In a tropical place like the Philippines, circumcision is necessary for personal hygiene as the closed foreskin could harbour germs that will lead to infection. Indeed, my husband got an infection when he lived in the Philippines.

In the Philippines, it's common for boys between the ages of 8 and 12 to be circumcised. These days, however, the procedure— cutting the foreskin covering the top part of the penis—is done soon after birth in most hospitals.

For older boys, summer is the best time to undergo this step into manhood. The World Health Organization (WHO) estimates that 30 per cent of males in the world aged 15 and above are circumcised, and around 70 per cent are Muslims. The practice is most prevalent in Muslim countries, Israel, South Korea, the United States and parts of Southeast Asia and Africa. It is rare I\in Europe, Latin America, parts of Southern Africa and most of Asia. It is done for several reasons: medical and hygienic purposes, religious ritual, and as a rite of passage for young boys, marking the beginning of their adulthood.

Then and Now

The early Muslim settlers, traders and proselytizers of Islam introduced circumcision to the natives of southern Philippines as part of their religious practice. At present, *pagtuli* (Filipino for 'circumcision') has become a tradition for Filipinos, regardless of religion.

Up until the 1980s (although some people say this is still prevalent today in rural areas), the procedure was carried out without anaesthesia. Armed with the basic requisites—guava leaves, a piece of wood called *lukaw*, a piece of cloth with a hole in the middle, and a razor—the local 'circumcision surgeon' would perform his duty for a pack of cigarettes or a bottle of the local gin, or sometimes even for free.

In places where there is a river, the boys would bathe while chewing on some guava leaves. Submerging their bodies in water would supposedly soften the skin, thus making it easier to cut. After

154

bathing, the boys stood in a queue by the riverbank where the 'surgeon' awaited them.

The foreskin was placed on top of the lukaw, and the razor positioned on top of the skin. A piece of wood would be used to push the razor to detach the foreskin from the penis. Some prefer the more traditional dorsal cut or slit where no tissue is removed. Sometimes, if the first boy in the queue cried in pain, some of the boys at the back would change their minds and go scurrying home.

After the procedure, each boy would spit out the chewed guava leaves on the wound to control the bleeding. To keep the tip of the penis exposed and to prevent the foreskin from growing back, it was inserted through the hole in the piece of cloth which was then wrapped around the shaft and secured with a string at the base. Water boiled with guava leaves and cooled down was used for cleaning the wound daily.

The newly circumcised boy is expected to be responsible for caring for his wound. He also has to endure being made fun of for wearing his mother's skirt while the wound is still fresh, an age-old ritual for the newly circumcised. It usually takes two weeks before he can resume his normal activities.

Most parents now prefer to have their boys circumcised by medical professionals who use anaesthesia in aseptic conditions, making the procedure much less traumatic and painful.

Breastfeeding and Sleeping

I wanted to breastfeed my baby, just as my mother breastfed me and my eight siblings. Unfortunately, this wasn't possible due to medical reasons. Thanks to my sister-in-law, Mary, I learned the basics of looking after my baby, including bottle-feeding and bathing him.

Mary taught me how to prepare my baby's trousseau. It was the first time I heard of babygrows, dummies and Calpol. I was also advised to allow my baby to cry and set a strict schedule for feeding and sleeping. Moreover, I was told to leave him at night to sleep in his own room.

I couldn't follow that last piece of advice. Even if we were just separated by a wall, the thought of not seeing him all night long was too much. In the Philippines, the infant is never left alone, much more so during the night! My husband, having lived in the Philippines, understood my dilemma. He had seen how Filipino parents always kept their babies by their side as much as possible.

This was how our two little ones ended up sleeping with us in our bedroom for four years. Having them so close was a source of great comfort and security for me.

24. IF I SING YOUR SONG, WILL YOU SING MINE?

'Music,' says the American musician Billy Joel, 'is an explosive expression of humanity. It's something we are all touched by, no matter what culture we're from.'

Music is a revelation of a person's innermost feeling, thoughts and fears, of their struggles and triumphs. There's always something anyone can relate to in a musical piece. This is why we sometimes find ourselves touched by a song. As we listen to the lyrics and melody of a song, we relive moments in our lives described by the song.

Remember the *kundiman*, those romantic Filipino songs with words and melodies that could melt a heart of stone? A kundiman usually portrays the forlorn pleas of a lover willing to sacrifice everything on behalf of their beloved. Some are plaintive calls of the rejected lover or the broken-hearted. Others tell the story of unrequited love. Almost all kundiman are heavy with poetic emotion. One such song about unrequited love is the classic Visayan song

'Matud Nila'.

We learn our favourite songs by heart and sing them to reveal our own feelings expressed so well by these songs. *'Ang Tangi Kong Pag-ibig', 'Dahil sa Iyo', 'Maalaala Mo Kaya?'* and *'Ay, Ay Kalisud'* are songs that have been passed from one generation to another, and whose appeal has never faded.

And who will ever forget our beloved folk songs like *'Magtanim ay di Biro', 'Bahay Kubo', 'Paruparong Bukid',* and *'Leron Leron Sinta'*— songs that make us nostalgic for the good old days and the comforts of home?

If music is the language of the soul, can it also be the language of integration?

Patrick and Noriana are very much into music. Both used to be members of an Irish traditional band called Nabac (which literally means 'not a bother').

In June 2006, the group was invited to perform at the celebration of the 108th Philippine Independence Day, attended by more than 3,000 newly arrived Filipinos and held at St. Anne's Park in Raheny, Dublin. The day was blessed by glorious sunshine, enabling parents and children and other guests to sit on the grass and rest under shady trees while being entertained. It was the first time most of them would hear Irish traditional music.

Armed with their instruments—Patrick on flute and bodhran, Noriana on tin whistle and vocals, Liz Coleman on violin, James

158

Ryan on guitar, mandolin and banjo, and Ciaran O'Donnell on flute and uilleann pipes—the band took to the stage and started playing. The audience was silent, trying to comprehend the foreign music, I would guess.

Each piece the band played was met with polite applause, but it was only when Noriana sang 'Ang Tangi Kong Pag-ibig' did a thunderous ovation and joyful approval emanate from the crowd.

Aha! If I sing your song, will you appreciate mine? This is how things go, of course. We are always flattered when foreigners speak some Filipino words, but it's a much bigger boost to our morale when they sing our songs!

It is at times like this when connections are established between two peoples. It was my husband, multicultural person that he was, who insisted that Noriana learn a Filipino song for this special occasion. He was right. We need to show attention to and love of the other. We need to welcome with open minds and hearts another people's culture. There are promising signs in our second generation of Irish Filipinos. Some of them have taken to Irish dancing; I'm pretty sure that in no time at all, they'll be playing Irish music as well.

The Filipino Musical Tradition

As a melting pot of different cultures, the Philippines has a diverse musical tradition blending eastern and western influences.

Traditional Philippine music features the indigenous music of prehistoric times (using instruments such as gongs and bamboo nose flutes) with music derived from the Spanish era. Both religious and secular Spanish influences are evident in the Tagalog kundiman, the Visayan *balitaw* and the Ilocano *dalot*. These different types of music share a certain naive sentimentality and melodious guitar accompaniments.

Muslim-Filipino groups, through their court and folk dance, have managed to preserve ancient Southeast Asian instruments and music. Their type of music usually tells a story. An example is the *'Singkil'*, a dance famous for its elegance and performed by other ethnic groups in the country. The Singkil relates an episode from the *Darangen* (the Maranao version of the ancient Indian epic, the Ramayana). The dance recounts the story of Putri Gandingan (Sita) as she was saved by Rajahmuda Bantugan (Rama) from crashing rocks, represented by bamboo poles.

The coming of the Americans changed the musical landscape in the Philippines. Lasting from 1898 to 1946, the American colonial regime institutionalised music as part of the educational curriculum. Filipino students in public schools learned vocal and instrumental performance, harmony counterpoint and composition—skills that they then used to create an independent Filipino musical tradition.

Music conservatories and colleges were also established. Here, students used their acquired musical skills to imitate western music and to create local versions of entire genres. Graduates from these institutions included the first generation of Filipino composers whose works were heavily western-influenced.

Americans introduced the blues, R&B, and rock and roll, which became popular genres in the Philippines. In the late 1950s, local musicians adapted Filipino lyrics for North American rock and roll music, resulting in the seminal origins of Philippine rock.

Up until the 1970s, popular Filipino rock musicians were writing and producing songs in English. In the early 1970s, however, rock groups like the Juan dela Cruz Band started writing Tagalog songs. Songs mixing English and Tagalog, also known as Taglish, also surfaced. Taglish was part of casual everyday speech, but using it in music was a bold move. The success of Taglish songs such as 'Mr DJ', Sharon Cuneta's first hit, made it a significant part of Filipino pop music.

Despite its history of being colonised for almost 400 years, the Philippines continues to take pride in its indigenous music, as shown in the vast Himig Collection of the Filipinas Heritage Library, which features more than 1,000 vinyl records of original Filipino music.

'Original Pilipino or Pinoy music (OPM)' used to refer to Filipino pop songs, especially those popularised from the 1970s through the mid-1990s. But the explosion of the alternative Filipino music scene in the 1990s that led to diverse musical styles made it necessary for the definition of OPM to extend to any type of original music created in the Philippines or composed by individuals of

Filipino extraction, regardless of location at the time the music was composed. The lyrics, in fact, may be in any language (although most are written in Tagalog, English or Taglish).

Irish Traditional Music

'Irish traditional music' is a very broad term that includes many different types of singing and instrumental music, spanning several time periods, as performed by Irish people in Ireland or outside of it, and occasionally nowadays by people of other nationalities.

While it incorporates a large body of material inherited from the past, Irish traditional music isn't static at all, but is constantly shedding material, reintroducing neglected items, composing new things and altering the performance of what's already established.

String, wind and free-reed melody instruments dominate Irish music, especially the fiddle, whistle, flute, uilleann pipes, concertina and accordion. Percussion instruments are also becoming more prominent.

Ireland may have produced world-famous musical acts such as U2 and The Script, but the Irish have a reverence for their traditional music. *Fleadh Cheoil na hÉireann* (the 'Music Festival of Ireland'), the world's biggest traditional Irish music celebration, still sees over 400,000 attendees each year, with dozens of nationalities arriving in Ireland to celebrate a 2,000-year-old musical tradition.

Irish music began as an oral tradition, passed on from generation to generation through merely listening and without being written down on paper. This is a practice that is still encouraged today—students of traditional music are taught to learn by ear and to pick up tunes that they hear from other people.

Traditional music saw a revival, especially in the U.S., in the 1920s when recordings of Irish music were taken for the first time and made available to the Irish migrants. The fiddler Michael Coleman's recordings in New York were to influence fiddlers in the States and in Ireland for many years to come.

A Musical Love Affair

There's so much more to learn about both Filipino and Irish music. It's a journey that's worth undertaking, because there's nothing like listening to and embracing music that speaks to your heart.

As adults, my children are still into music. What was once a hobby has turned into a livelihood for both of them. More importantly, though, is that music continues to be a source of joy and relaxation for them. My son married a Frenchwoman who's also a musician. My daughter is also married to a fellow musician. Through music, they and their partners have found and shown other people a way to love and live harmoniously, no matter the differences in their language, skin colour, politics and faith.

25. THE 'GREENING' OF THE BROWN PEOPLE

'Patrick' is the most versatile name on the planet. A Patrick can also be called Pat, Pad, Podge, Packie, Padpad, Patching or Phadraig. These are the nicknames that my son accumulated through the years. We named him after his granddad, as tradition dictates, and after Saint Patrick, Ireland's national patron saint.

Choosing my son's name was a rite of passage for me. Giving him an Irish name was my baptism into Irishness, of turning 'green' and becoming one with my new community.

There's a famous St Patrick's Day ad campaign by Tourism Ireland that showed several international landmarks—the Great Wall of China, Christ the Redeemer in Brazil, the ancient Rock of Petra in Jordan, the Sleeping Beauty's Castle at Disneyland Paris, and many other famous spots—turning 'green' for a day. Although I didn't turn a literal green like the landmarks in the adverts, I had become green in spirit in the sense that I had now embraced Ireland as my second home and country. With this, I also made space in my heart for other cultures—Polish, Chinese, Indian, Nigerian—people from other countries who, like me, had come to love our new home.

The 17th of March marks the day we honour St Patrick and the very challenging circumstances under which he arrived on this island. A Roman-Briton who came to Ireland as a slave, Patrick forgave his captors and accepted the Irish he encountered as his own community. 'It was this generous spirit,' said President Michael D. Higgins in his 2014 message, 'that commended Patrick to be embraced as our beloved patron saint. His name has since become synonymous with an inclusive and authentic version of Irishness with its stress on the duty and the joys of hospitality.'

Filipinos have been fortunate enough to receive Irish hospitality. In Dublin, for instance, the young members of Filipino community in Crumlin were the recipients of the St Patrick's Festival community outreach programme. City Fusion for the over-18s and Brighter Futures for those in the 12–18 age group are two projects that promote diversity and inclusion by letting the programme recipients work with professional artists in creating two large-scale pageants for the Festival parade.

St Patrick was a migrant, and Ireland's ethnic mix is never more evident than in every St Patrick's Day celebration. In recent years, there has been a welcome increase in the number and variety of St. Patrick's Day celebrations, facilitating greater participation by the diverse communities that make up the tapestry of our country.

The many parades that now take place across the country express people's pride in their new home. They are, as confirmed by President Higgins, 'valuable expressions of community solidarity and are deserving of our participation and support.'

For several thousand naturalised Irish-Filipino citizens, this is the best time to show their 'Irishness', to express their unity and support by actively participating in the local festival.

For many years, the Filipino community in Cork have participated in the parade with their vibrant street dance, '*Dinagyang*', and traditional Filipino costumes. This dynamic presentation is always a big attraction. Victoria Magday, United Filipino Association (UFIA) President, said, 'This is a showcase of our culture, depicting traditions from [the] three major regions in the Philippines—Luzon, Visayas and Mindanao. The theme is celebrating our Philippine connection with the Irish and other nationalities.'

The Limerick Filipino community had won the Most Entertaining Group award with their lively performance of Filipino folk dances and colourful attires. St Patrick's Festival in Galway has a carnival atmosphere and a great showcase for the diversity of its community. The Galway Filipino community's performance was a big surprise in 2014 when several Filipinas dressed in tri-colour costumes walked about, twirling green, white and orange parasols. They drew the loudest cheers from the spectators.

By becoming involved with the community and taking part in

Irish celebrations, the Filipino community are putting their best foot forward towards integration. By valuing their own heritage and connecting it with the larger Irish society, they are building friendship, trust and respect with the other cultures in the country.

26. I AM SORRY FOR YOUR TROUBLE

I went to my first funeral in Ireland in 1983 when my mother-in-law, Nora Lande, died at the age of 86. During the wake, people stood in a queue to condole with the bereaved. I was struck by the whispers of 'I'm sorry for your trouble' from the sympathisers as they shook hands with members of the family.

'I'm sorry for your trouble' used to be a formal expression of sympathy in Ireland. Like many local traditions, however, it's no longer practised these days. For really, what better way to show sympathy to the bereaved than to give them a warm hug, some comforting words or a tight handshake? Even without saying a word, one's presence at a funeral is enough to comfort a grieving person.

'Wake' is an interesting word. To wake means to be ready to get up and start the day, but in the context of mourning, a wake is keeping vigil over the dead before the burial. The wake, the glorious send-off of departed loved ones, was once a prominent feature of Irish funeral traditions, but we see less and less of it in modern Ireland.

The speed of funerals in Ireland (most people are buried within two days) means that radio stations read out the local death notices every day, usually twice or three times a day, as it would be too late to have them published in the weekly local paper.

Funerals can be held during the day or in the evening. In an evening funeral, the coffin is taken from the funeral parlour to the church, where a short liturgy is said. In my local parish in Lucan, mourners are afterwards invited by the parish hospitality group for a cup of tea or coffee, and scones in the parish centre. This gives them another opportunity to condole with the bereaved.

The funeral takes place the next morning with Holy Mass and followed either by burial in the cemetery or cremation. Relations and friends who travelled from afar are always invited by the bereaved to have lunch with them in a nearby hotel or restaurant.

In the Philippines, a wake (called *lamay*) typically lasts for five to seven nights, but may last longer if there are loved ones who will be travelling from afar. During the wake, the deceased, placed in a coffin, is displayed in their house or a funeral parlour.

Family members, relatives and acquaintances participate in the vigil. Apart from offering condolences, mourners also give abuloy (financial donations) to help defray funeral and burial costs. The lamay is also an occasion to celebrate, and food and drinks are normally served every evening. It's not unusual to find mourners singing, playing the guitar, and even playing cards or mah-jong to

170

pass the time and to keep awake. The Catholic orientation of the Filipinos allows them to take death as an ordinary, even communal, experience.

Marie Murray, an Irish psychologist, has this to say about the relevance of funerals:

'Funeral attendance is a statement of connection, care, compassion and support. It encircles those who grieve and enriches those who attend because it connects each person there to the profundity of living and the inevitability of death. Funeral attendees witness the raw emotions of grief and the extraordinary capacity of the human spirit to love.'

'Each time we attend a funeral we confront our own mortality. If we have not yet experienced personal loss we are made aware of the emotions and rituals that surround it and the sacredness of sorrow. If the territory of death is familiar to us then resonances are evoked and we have the chance to revisit our own remembrance of others who have died.... there is psychological reason, social solidarity and cultural cohesion in funeral attendance, and even as the ceremonies, the belief systems they operate from or the expression of grief may change, the meaning of marking death remains, and long may we travel highway and byway to do so.'

27. RELAX, HAVE A CUP OF TEA

In the Philippines, tea is just an ordinary drink that can relieve a stomach ailment or quench thirst. But on my arrival in Ireland, I discovered that tea is something the Irish can't live without. Here, it's known as the cup that cheers, the drink of friendship and camaraderie.

Tea is taken so seriously in Ireland that President John F. Kennedy being served tea by his cousin Mary Ryan in the courtyard of her modest farmhouse in Ireland in 1963 is considered the true moment of homecoming for the U.S. president. This moment in history was celebrated on a commemorative stamp issued in 2013.

Ireland is the largest tea consumer per capita in the world. You won't find a convention, work meeting or any other event that doesn't include a morning or afternoon tea break in its schedule. Tea and biscuit is the go-to refreshment when friends or neighbours call at home. Some cautionary advice though. It's still important to know your visitors—if they're the sort of person who loves a tipple, it's still best to give them a shot of whiskey or a glass of wine.

Tea was first imported into Ireland in 1835 and promptly became popular with the wealthy class. But it wasn't until later in the mid-1800s that it reached rural people. After that, all of Ireland was hooked. Small grocers opened in the towns and villages, where people exchanged butter and eggs for tea and sugar.

The Irish make a strong cup. Irish tea is blended to be mixed with milk. Irish breakfast tea is often a strong blend of Assam and Ceylon, and most people use this blend all day long. Even at a traditional Irish wake, it's expected that a pot would be continuously boiling to make tea for company.

You might think that making tea is a casual thing but, as I found out from my husband, there's a method to making a proper cup of tea that leaves the drinker satisfied. I now follow this process suggested by tea taster Dominic Witherow:

What you'll need:

- A kettle
- Tea: Either bags or loose leaves will do.
- A teapot: A lot of people tend to overlook this, but it really is essential. A china one is perfect.
- A mug for daily use, a cup for social occasions
- Milk: This is important if you want to get the true flavour of tea, but drinking your tea black is also acceptable.
- Sugar (optional)
- Cake or biscuits (optional, but desirable)

Method:

1. Put enough water in your kettle to fill the teapot, plus a bit more to warm it.

2. Start boiling the water.

3. When the water gets hot, but not boiling yet, pour a bit into the teapot and swill it around. This will serve to warm the pot, so that the pot doesn't end up cooling the water while the tea is brewing. Don't skip this part, as the tea might not brew properly if the pot is too cold. Just before the water boils—you can tell that it's close to boiling when the steam gets heavier and you start to hear bubbling sounds—empty the teapot and place one teabag or a heaped spoon of leaves in the pot.

4. As soon as the water boils, pour it into the teapot. The water should be seething as it's poured, as the heat will help draw the flavour out of the leaves to mix with the water. Put the lid on the pot and let the tea brew—3 to 5 minutes should be long enough. You can check the colour of the tea—it should be a rich brown but you should still be able to see through to the bottom of the pot.

5. Once the tea is brewed, you can pour it into the cup or mug. China retains flavour well, so it's best to use this type of vessel. Some people pour the milk into the cup before the tea, but it makes more sense to pour the tea first. This way, you can see better how strong the tea is as you pour the milk.

6. Add the desired amount of sugar (or none at all), then stir the tea well. Tea is best served with a classic cake, such as Victoria sponge, but biscuits are nice too.

7. Now that your tea's ready, let the good times and easy conversations begin. Just sit back, relax and let the cares of the world drift away. This is how you serve a proper cup of Irish tea.

Tea Is a Meal

Did you know that 'tea' also means a meal in Ireland? Soon after I arrived in Ireland, while visiting a relative of my husband, I was called for tea at 5 p.m. I politely declined as I wasn't thirsty. I didn't realise they were actually telling me that supper was being served. I ended up going to bed hungry that night.

So here's a rundown of the tea-related meals served in Ireland, just so you don't end up missing meals like I did:

Elevenses is served, as the name suggests, at 11.00 a.m. Tea is served with scones and biscuits. This morning meal should hold you over until lunch.

Afternoon tea is served between 3.00 and 5.00 p.m. It is the equivalent of the Filipino merienda. Here you serve light, sweet items with tea.

High tea is served at 5.00 or 6.00 p.m. It's also called supper or dinner, depending on which part of the country you're in. You serve much more substantial fare with this tea, such as meat or fish, bread and fruit. In the summer, cold meats and salads are served with the tea to suit the weather.

Tea and Literature

Writing and tea go together so well. How many famous literary quotes have been borne out of tea?

'You can never get a cup of tea large enough or a book long enough to suit me.'

—**CS Lewis**

'I say let the world go to hell, but I should always have my tea.'

—**Fyodor Dostoyevsky**, *Notes from Underground*

'I shouldn't think even millionaires could eat anything nicer than new bread and real butter and honey for tea.'

—**Dodie Smith**, *I Capture the Castle*

'In Ireland, you go to someone's house, and she asks you if you want a cup of tea. You say no, thank you, you're really just fine. She asks if you're sure. You say of course you're sure, really, you don't need a thing. Except they pronounce it ting. You don't need a ting. Well, she says then, I was going to get myself some anyway, so it would be no trouble. Ah, you say, well, if you were going to get yourself some, I wouldn't mind a spot of tea, at that, so long as it's no trouble and I can give you a hand in the kitchen. Then you go through the whole thing all over again until you both end up in the kitchen drinking tea and chatting.

'In America, someone asks you if you want a cup of tea, you say no, and then you don't get any damned tea.

'I liked the Irish way better.'

—**CE Murphy**, *Urban Shaman*

'When tea becomes ritual, it takes its place at the heart of our ability to see greatness in small things. Where is beauty to be found? In great things that, like everything else, are doomed to die, or in small things that aspire to nothing, yet know how to set a jewel of infinity in a single moment?'

—**Muriel Barbery**, *The Elegance of the Hedgehog*

'There are few hours in life more agreeable than the hour dedicated to the ceremony known as afternoon tea.'

—**Henry James,** *The Portrait of a Lady*

'If you are cold, tea will warm you;
if you are too heated, it will cool you;
If you are depressed, it will cheer you;
If you are excited, it will calm you.'

—**William Ewart Gladstone**

'A woman is like a tea bag; you never know how strong it is until it's in hot water.'

—**Eleanor Roosevelt**

'Thank God for tea! What would the world do without tea! How did it exist? I am glad I was not born before tea.'

— **Sydney Smith,** *A Memoir of the Reverend Sydney Smith*

28. THE CASE OF THE UNSPOKEN IRISH LANGUAGE

We Filipinos are perplexed by our own identity. We have emerged from our colonial episodes to engage in a confused, sometimes futile search for a national identity. We are caught between cultural influences from our Malay origins, Spanish colonisation and Americanisation.

Despite all these, though, we have maintained and developed our national language and kept our regional dialects. Hundreds of years of colonisation didn't take away our love for our native tongue, even if English is our second language.

I'm saying this because of the Irish situation. In spite of having lived in Ireland for almost 40 years, I have only learned a few words of Irish. If I lived in France, Italy or Spain for that same number of years, I would no doubt be speaking the local language fluently by now.

Irish is the first language of the country, according to the Irish

Constitution. It is one of the official languages of the EC, yet only a few people speak the language well. These are the figures, as listed by Anthony Bluett in his book *Things Irish*, which was published in 1994: There are about 30,000 genuine native Irish speakers left, and maybe 50,000 people who use the language on a day-to-day basis. About a million people have "some knowledge" of Irish. 'Attitudes among the citizens of Ireland to their language differ,' Bluett says, 'but most people just don't seem to have an attitude. They don't care.'

Irish was spoken by almost everyone in Ireland until the end of the 16th century. By the 18th century, the Irish-speaking aristocracy, learned class and their institutions had been replaced by a new English-speaking, land-owning class and an English-speaking middle-class in the growing towns. Irish remained only the language of the poor labouring class. Anyone who wanted to climb up the social ladder had to speak English.

Mass emigration after the great famine contributed to the demise of the Irish language. The structure of rural society changed, and a whole class of mainly Irish speakers disappeared, and with them went the language, culture and folk traditions of centuries.

In the years that followed, the educational system improved, but it was also largely to blame for the disappearance of the Irish language, as schools were established exclusively in English. The powerful Catholic Church had now been given an administrative right to exist in Ireland, but the hierarchy took little interest in promoting the native language.

179

At the end of the 19th century, there was a revival of interest in Irish, at the same time as the Nationalist movement gained a certain amount of credibility in middle-class circles. 'But,' according to Bluett, 'this revival among people who had never spoken the language anyway was often just a sort of fashionable flirtation with the idea of being Irish, and certainly did nothing to revive the language in its native context.'

Irish was given a privileged place in the educational system, being made a compulsory subject. You had to have learned Irish to gain entrance to university (with the exception of Trinity College) and a wide range of public sector jobs. But Irish still wasn't used in ordinary life. As Fiona Griffin concludes in her 1991 book *Why Do the Irish?:*

> 'Unfortunately the methods of teaching don't often make them love the language, and they usually have no motivation to speak it at home or with their friends.'

Bluett is more blunt:

> 'They approached it as if it were something dug up intact after a thousand years submerged in an airtight bog: perfect but dead.'

Sadly, today, the Irish language is seen as a tolerated burden, something you have to learn to pass your exams, get a job or get into college, but which you can ditch afterwards, as it's not really useful anyway in the real world.

PART FOUR
DISCOVER CULTURAL
INTEGRATION

'We don't need a melting pot in this country, folks. We need a salad bowl. In a salad bowl, you put in the different things. You want the vegetables—the lettuce, the cucumbers, the onions, the green peppers—to maintain their identity. You appreciate differences.'

—Jane Elliott

29. EAT YOUR WAY

Marrying an Irishman and settling down in Ireland meant that I would unconditionally accept the country, its people and its food. My gastronomic journey has been really interesting, as I learned a new way of cooking and eating.

In 1977, to eat Asian food, you needed a fine comb to find an Asian shop or a Chinese take-away in Dublin. There's little time to explore, however, when you're adjusting to the byways and highways of a new country. I therefore had to prepare myself for the inevitable.

Food has always been a comfort blanket for Filipinos—we need to have food in sight to feel secure. When Filipino food is hard to find, what do you do? Sulk and go hungry? I knew I couldn't do this, so I mustered my energy and told myself that I had no choice but to eat Irish food.

It was extremely hard initially. When you've lived most of your life eating rice with fish, chicken, pork and beef cooked the Filipino way, how long will it take you to get used to eating bacon and cabbage, roast, stews, ham and fish fingers, or having a full Irish breakfast? How would it feel to replace rice with potatoes?

I was blessed to have stayed with my sister-in-law, Mary, for a few weeks. Watching her cook and tasting her dishes made me realise, to my delight, that I love Irish food—from full Irish breakfast to baked beef and bacon. Most of all, I discovered that Irish dishes are a lot easier to cook! There's little chopping and sautéing to do. There are basically three ways of cooking—boiling, roasting and frying. There's no hurry as it takes two to three hours (depending on the weight of the meat) to boil or roast beef, ham and bacon. This gives you plenty of time to do other things while waiting for your food to cook.

Tourism Ireland might promote the full Irish version with soda bread, sausages, rashers and fried eggs, but on an ordinary day, most Irish people have the typical tea and toast with cereal for breakfast. Once home after work, they would heartily dig into a dinner consisting of a chunk of meat with potatoes and one or two root vegetables, such as carrots, parsnips or swedes. This satisfying meal keeps one full through the night and even the next day. There's no need for snacks of crisps and sweets during the day.

Potato: The Irish Staple

As we Filipinos are fussy with rice, so are the Irish over their potatoes. Typically, a supermarket will stock at least five or six varieties, depending on the season, and each suited to a particular method of cooking.

Preparing a great potato dish doesn't have to be difficult; it can be as simple as throwing them in the oven with some butter and salt. The hardest part, in fact, is often making sure you buy the right **type** of potato as there are about 5,000 varieties worldwide!

With the arrival of foods from around the world in our supermarkets, potato production is changing as well. It remains an essential crop in Europe (especially eastern and central Europe), where per capita production is still the highest in the world, but the most rapid expansion over the past few decades has occurred in southern and eastern Asia. China now leads the world in potato production, and nearly a third of the world's potatoes are harvested in China and India. With the production of rice getting more and more complicated, it is possible that someday Filipinos may have potatoes as their staple food too!

Bacon and Cabbage: The Most Popular Dish in Ireland

Fellow Filipinos in Ireland, if you have been in Ireland for ten years or longer, but have not cooked or even tasted bacon and cabbage, shame on you. You should be curious about the most popular dish in Ireland, served to visiting friends and relations from abroad. In many homes across the world, particularly on St. Patrick's Day, people of Irish descent enjoy this dish as a 'taste of home'. I remember an Irish friend from America who was treated to a bacon-and-cabbage dinner every day by different relations on her five-day visit to Ireland!

The name 'bacon' means different things in different parts of the world. To clarify: Bacon as used in this dish is a 'cured' joint taken from the shoulder or the back of a pig. Bacon in America is usually taken from the belly of the pig. So, if you want to replicate the dish as closely as possible, ask your butcher for a shoulder of pork or pork loin.

Here is the recipe:

Bacon and Cabbage

Serves 12–15

Ingredients:

2.25 kg (5 lbs) loin, collar or streaky bacon, either smoked or unsmoked, with the rind on and a nice covering of fat

1 Savoy or 2 spring cabbages

50 g (2 oz) butter

freshly ground pepper

parsley sauce (see recipe)

In a large pot, cover the bacon with cold water and slowly bring it to the boil. If the bacon is very salty, there will be a white froth on top of the water as it boils. If this happens, discard the water and start again.

You might need to do this several times, depending on how salty the bacon is. Once you've gotten rid of the froth, cover the bacon with hot water, cover the pot and let it simmer until it's almost cooked. Allow around 20 minutes for every kilogram of meat (2.2 lbs).

Meanwhile, trim the cabbage and cut it into quarters. Remove the hard core of the cabbage. Shred the cabbage, and if necessary, wash it in cold water. Around 20 minutes before the end of the cooking time for the bacon, add the shredded cabbage. Stir it into the boiling water, cover the pot, and continue to boil the mixture gently until both the bacon and cabbage are done.

Take the bacon out. Strain the cabbage and discard the water (or, if it's not too salty, save it for soup). Add a lump of butter to the cabbage. Season with lots of ground pepper; it's unlikely to need more salt, but add some if necessary. Serve the bacon with the cabbage, parsley sauce and floury potatoes.

Parsley Sauce (optional)

600 ml (1 pint) cold full-cream milk
a few parsley stalks
sprig of thyme
a few slices of carrot (optional)
a few slices of onion (optional)
salt and freshly ground pepper
about 50 g (2 oz) curly parsley, freshly chopped
50 g of roux prepared by melting 25 g of butter and adding 25 of plain
  flour to it, until a thick white paste is formed

Pour the milk into a saucepan, and add the herbs and vegetables. Heat the mixture until it starts boiling, season and simmer for 4–5 minutes. Strain the milk, then bring it back to the boil and whisk in the roux until the sauce takes on a light consistency. Season again with salt and freshly ground pepper. Add the chopped parsley and simmer on a very low heat for 4 to 5 minutes. Taste and correct the seasoning.

30. SING YOUR WAY

While many Filipinos toil anonymously as nurses and doctors, maids, sailors, construction workers and labourers in foreign countries, would you believe that tens of thousands of them stand in the spotlight, entertaining crowds as singers and musicians?

Filipino entertainers cut across all tastes, from the sacred choral music of the Madrigal Singers to the edgy alternative music of the Eraserheads and Rivermaya, all considered as legendary Filipino musicians.

But the country's best-known musical export is probably Lea Salonga, a famous musical entertainer in Manila long before the rest of the world embraced her. Lea made her professional debut at the age of seven in the Repertory Philippines production of *The King and I*. At the age of 10, she began her recording career and received a gold record in the Philippines for her first album, *Small Voice*.

As a teenager, she established herself as a pop singer and actress, but a fortuitous break came when she was chosen to open for Stevie Wonder at a concert. Word of her precocious talent spread, and after rigorous auditions, she was offered the role of Kim in the London

188

West End production of *Miss Saigon*. It was the role that would make her famous worldwide, and for which she won the Olivier, Tony, Drama Desk, Outer Critics and Theatre World awards.

Salonga was the first Filipino artist to be signed to an international record label in 1993, and to have received a major album release and distribution deal in the U.S. (The second one was Charice Pempengco). She's one of the best-selling Filipino artists of all time, with her album sales going over 5 million worldwide.

There's a huge demand for Filipino performers abroad, according to Jackson Gan, a talent agent and head of a music recording studio in Manila. Gan estimates that between 25,000 and 30,000 Filipino musicians and singers perform in around 3,000 clubs, hotels, cruise ships and restaurants around the world at any one time. He says even Malaysian, Indonesian, Australian and Chinese bands tend to recruit Filipino lead singers.

Gan attributes the success of Filipino performers overseas to the roles music and dance play in Filipino culture. Singing contests are often the highlights of fiestas and beauty contests, while live television shows are centred on song-and-dance numbers. Karaoke is one of the country's most popular forms of entertainment, with guests at weddings and birthday parties expected to belt out songs behind a microphone to entertain their hosts and fellow guests.

When in Ireland, what do Filipinos do? Sing, of course. A karaoke machine is always a standby at home not only to while away the blues but to hone vocal skills and entertain party guests as well.

How many Filipino church choirs and groups do we have in Ireland? At least one in every county. Filipinos compete in TV song competitions like *The Voice* where you normally get one or two Filipino contestants every season. But the most popular among the Irish Filipinos was Pinoy Idol, which was set up in Dublin in 2000 to cater to a bustling group of Filipinos who loved to sing. It lasted for 15 years. The programme originated from Pop Idol, a television franchise created by British entertainment executive Simon Fuller. Pop Idol sought to discover the best singer or 'idol' in the country through a series of auditions followed by live performances.

Irish Songs and Music

My first exposure to Irish music was in a pub. Seated comfortably with a drink in one hand and chatting away with friends, I noticed the gradual entrance of a group of people carrying musical instruments. All of them gathered in a corner in the room. After a drink or two, somebody in the group started beating a bodhran, while another started playing a banjo. A few moments later someone else joined in with another instrument, and voila, in no time at all, the whole pub was bursting with music!

I found out that this is what the Irish call a music session, an informal gathering where people play traditional music. The Irish word for 'session' is *seisiún*, which can also refer to a singing session

190

or a mixed session (a mixture of tunes and songs) held in traditional Irish music pubs, where musicians of all kinds get together for joint sessions. Anyone who wants to can join in spontaneously while observing some rules.

The general session scheme is that someone starts a tune, and those who know it join in. Good session etiquette requires not playing if one does not know the tune, and waiting until a tune one knows comes along. In an 'open' session, anyone who can play Irish music is welcome.

Most often there are more-or-less recognised session leaders; sometimes there are no leaders at all. At times a song will be sung or a slow air played by a single musician between sets.

The objective in a session is not to provide music for an audience of passive listeners, although punters (non-playing attendees) often come just to listen. The session is a shared experience to be enjoyed by the musicians themselves, not a performance that's sold to an audience. Some people contend that the session is the main sphere where music is composed and innovated. Sessions also enable less advanced musicians to practise in a group setting.

The choice of music can be described as 'pot luck', depending on the musicians' instrumental proficiency, their ability to play together and the general mood. Some sessions might encourage its audience to dance to lively jigs, or move them to tears from sad ballads. They might even compel the audience to just finish their drinks and head home. Thankfully, this doesn't happen often.

Musical instruments are the heart of most sessions, and singing is normally relegated to second fiddle. The music also tends to be experimental rather than familiar.

The more regular a session is advertised, the more modern or the larger the venue, and the more urban the area, the more likely that the session is a 'professional' one. This means that the musicians were especially hired by the landlord to provide entertainment, instead of coming together randomly. In this case, you can expect popular music to be played. Some venues also throw in some Irish dancing or a group of singers. Whatever the sessions may consist of, they're always better than the piped-in music that you'd normally get in upscale, hip pubs.

Socially, sessions have often been compared to an evening of playing card games, where the conversation and camaraderie are an essential component. In many rural communities in Ireland, sessions are an integral part of community life.

Sunday afternoons and week nights (especially Tuesday and Wednesday) are common times for sessions to be scheduled in pubs, on the theory that these are the least likely times for dances and concerts to be held, and therefore the times that professional musicians will be most able to show.

Sessions can also be held in homes or at various public places in addition to pubs. For instance, you can often have sessions in a beer tent or in the vendor's booth of a music-loving craftsman at a music festival. When a particularly large musical event 'takes over' an entire village, spontaneous sessions may erupt on the street corners. Sessions may also take place occasionally at wakes, or in a house party or any other occasion where musicians are gathered.

31. DRINK YOUR WAY

Do you think the Irish drink too much? Believe it or not, Filipinos could outdrink anyone in the world, apart from the South Koreans and Russians. Euromonitor, an international research firm, revealed in a 2013 survey that a Filipino adult drinks an average of 5.4 shots of distilled alcohol weekly, making the country third on the list of the world's heaviest drinkers.

South Koreans rank first, averaging 13.7 shots per week. Russians are second, with 6.3 shots per adult a week. Despite its reputation for heavy drinking, Ireland was only 17th on the list, with 2.6 shots per week.

Filipinos have a peculiar way of drinking. A group share one glass which is passed around in a circle. The glass is filled up by a *tanggero* whose job is to put liquor in the glass and remember whose turn it is.

Drinking in a circle and sharing the glass is a sign of fraternity and equality among the group. Most Fillipinos can't afford expensive alcohol, but this doesn't stop them from having their drinking sessions with friends. They're happy to settle for the most affordable drink—what matters most is the camaraderie that comes from sharing the drink.

The most affordable local drink is the *lambanog* ('coconut whiskey'). Similiar to the Irish poitin made from potatoes, lambanog is known for its potency (it is sold in 80- or 90-proof varieties). It is primarily produced in Quezon and popular among farmers.

The process begins with the coconut tree, 'the tree of life'. As with most fruit-bearing trees, coconut flowers turn into fruit. However lambanog-making trees never produce fruit, because it is the sap from the coconut flower that is the crucial ingredient for this unique coconut wine. Plantation workers called *mangagarit* climb the trees every afternoon to prune the flowers so that their sap drips into bamboo receptacles called *tukil*. (This process is similar to tapping a rubber tree.) The next morning, the mangagarit return to collect the sap from the tukil. The sap is then put through a cooking or fermentation process, which produces coconut toddy called *tuba*. The tuba is then taken and distilled to produce lambanog. Until recently, lambanog was primarily a local drink, much like homemade apple cider or backwoods moonshine.

For Filipinos, a drinking session isn't complete without *pulutan*. Pulutan, like the Spanish *tapas*, are finger foods taken to stave-off drunkenness. Filipinos overseas can easily concoct pulutan from a quick visit to an Asian grocery—one of the most common dishes is called 'tuna skyflake.' It's made from crushing a few pieces of Skyflakes—a famous brand of savoury crackers—and mixing them with tinned tuna. Another favourite pulutan is *chicharon* or pork crackling, usually dipped in vinegar mixed with chillies.

The Perfect Irish Pint

Drinking cultures vary from place to place. It's good to acquaint yourself with the terminology of Irish pub culture: pub, publican, bartender, pull a pint, pub grub, session, *cráic*, the local. Without a skilled bartender, pouring or pulling the 'perfect pint' (a pint is a unit of liquid or dry capacity equal to one-eighth of a gallon or around 568 ml) might end up being not so perfect in its presentation for the customer's appreciation.

'Pub' is short for 'public house.' The person who runs a pub is called a 'publican.' All pubs offer beer, but the most important thing for a pub to provide is *cráic* ('crack')—that's Irish for a jolly good time.

Pubs play a very important role in Irish life. The Irish pub is a refuge for camaraderie and friendship. But pub culture goes far more than that. For the last century, the Irish public house has been a social and community centre for the people of Ireland. It functions as both a place to consume alcohol at leisure and one in which to meet with friends, neighbours and complete strangers, in order to converse in a relaxed atmosphere. Feasts are celebrated here—weddings, funerals (the wake), christenings, birthdays and every other celebration you could think of.

Most Irish people will have a 'local', which is the pub that they frequent most often. There is generally a close relationship between the customer and the bar staff and, in many cases, particularly in country pubs, virtually all of the customers will know each other very well. Indeed, a barman asking a local what he'd like to drink would be like asking him what his name was. Ireland is home to more than 10,000 pubs so you won't have to travel far to go for a pint. Pubs are important points of social encounters, where people from all social ranks get together.

One thing that often surprises visitors is the presence of children in Irish pubs. The drinking age in Ireland is eighteen, but it's legal for children under that age to enter with their families for lunch or dinner. Pub food, or 'pub grub', is generally inexpensive and hearty. While almost any pub can be expected to provide sandwiches or maybe even baked potatoes, some pubs have become famous for their food. The Reginald in Waterford, The Stag's Head in Dublin and Langton's in Kilkenny are good places to visit for culinary experiences.

A significant recent change to pub culture in the country is the implementation of the smoking ban in all workplaces, including pubs and restaurants. Ireland was the first country in the world to implement such a ban, which was introduced on 29 March 2004. A majority of the population support the ban, including a significant percentage of smokers. Nevertheless, the atmosphere in pubs has changed greatly as a result, and debate continues on whether it has boosted or lowered sales, although this is often blamed on the ever-increasing prices, or whether it is a 'good thing' or a 'bad thing'. A similar ban under the Smoking (Northern Ireland) Order 2006 came into effect in Northern Ireland on 30 April 2007.

Pubs are the place to go for traditional music or 'trad', as the locals call it. Larger places might have professional bands, but the most common format is the session, as described in Chapter 30. The musicians in a session are usually playing for beer only, so there generally isn't a cover charge. The pubs in Doolin. Co. Clare are famous for their trad.

Here's some cautionary advice: When someone invites you to a pub in Ireland, it is common practice for them to purchase the first drink, and for you to order the next. Make sure to order the next drink before your companion finishes theirs to keep the camaraderie going, and remember, it is never necessary to 'tip' bar staff.

A 'round' refers to the set of drinks purchased by one person in a group for the whole group. The purchaser buys the round of drinks as a single order at the bar. In many places, it is customary for people to take turns buying rounds.

32. MARRY YOUR WAY

Would you be happy to live in a country where divorce isn't legal?

Apart from the Vatican, the Philippines is the only state in the world without divorce laws. Only Muslims in the Philippines can file for divorce, as they are governed by the Code of Muslim Personal Laws. There's been a growing clamour from women who are trapped in loveless marriages, or have been entirely abandoned by their husbands, for divorce to be legalised in the country. Believe it or not, divorce used to be legal in the Philippines under the American colonial regime, although it was only allowed on the grounds of adultery or concubinage. The Japanese, who occupied the country between 1942 and 1945, introduced more liberal divorce laws. Divorce only became illegal when the Philippine Civil Code of 1949, modelled after the strongly Catholic Spanish Civil Code, was enacted.

Current laws allow for legal separation, which lets a couple live apart, but not marry new partners. Worse, they could be jailed for adultery or concubinage if they get caught with another partner.

199

The only recourse is to file for annulment. A marriage can only be declared null if it involves bigamy, incest, mistaken identity or polygamy, if the marriage licence isn't valid, or at least one of the couple was a minor when they got married.

Annulment is a long and costly process that most Filipinos can't afford. It costs around $400 just to file for annulment, but legal costs can go up to $10,000. In a country where a quarter of the population earn less than $200 a month, annulment is an impossible recourse for most. Furthermore, it can take years of investigation and traumatic court interrogations before a decision can be made on the validity of a marriage.

Still, thousands of petitions to end marriages are filed every year, mostly by women. Many end up being denied. Many stories have been written about couples who have grown apart but cannot move on with their new lives, and women whose husbands had abandoned them but cannot marry their new partners. There are many traumatic tales about court hearings, where a petitioner has to recount every little incident to prove that their marriage shouldn't be valid anymore, only to be told that there isn't enough evidence for their spouse's infidelity or psychological incapacity.

Despite the growing number of Filipinos who are in favour of the enactment of a divorce law in the country, the proposal keeps getting turned down by political leaders who are mostly Catholic. As of 2016, the leading women's rights political party, Gabriela, has proposed a divorce bill five times. Unfortunately, even if the

Philippine Constitution clearly states that the State should be separate from the Church, the Church continues to exert a lot of influence on the decisions made by the country's most powerful politicians and the divorce bill doesn't look like it will be passed anytime soon.

Divorced Ireland

Here in Ireland, it's been over 20 years since the Irish public voted to have divorce legalised. In the referendum held in November 1995, 51 per cent voted for the country to remove the constitutional ban on divorce. Legislation followed in June 1996.

The campaign leading to the referendum was extremely divisive, which isn't surprising because, like the Philippines, Ireland is a predominantly Catholic country.

In her campaign to persuade women to vote Yes, then minister of state at the Department of Foreign Affairs Joan Burton pleaded for 'the small voice of honesty and truthfulness, however painful' and asserted that civil divorce was 'a more honourable and honest process' than annulment, which declared that the marriage had never existed at all.

At the final conference by the anti-divorce campaigners before the referendum, Prof William Binchy warned that 'the proposed amendment would remove constitutional protection from the first family in favour of the second partner following a divorce.'

Binchy went on to say that legalising divorce would 'reward deserters, leaving abandoned wives in a perilous financial position; that it would require the premature sale of the family home or business; and that it would enable quickie divorces by allowing a divorce to be obtained when the spouses were still living in the same home.' He also said that men who had deserted their wives would be able to claim the family assets and leave their wives in poverty.

'Hello divorce, bye-bye, Daddy' read some of the anti-divorce posters, implying that legalising divorce would lead to fathers abandoning their families.

To be fair to the No campaigners, some of the things they had warned about did come to pass—divorce has plunged some families into poverty, some people have been forced to sell their homes, and some women have, out of bitterness, denied visitation rights to their ex-husbands.

But in the end, the Irish people decided that the best thing to do was face the reality that many marriages have broken down, and are likely to do so in the future. This isn't to say that the legalisation of divorce has led them to make a habit of jumping from one marriage to another. In fact, in all of Europe, Ireland has the lowest divorce rate, and is the third lowest in the world, just behind Mexico and Chile.

33. WORSHIP GOD YOUR WAY

A church is always the first port of call for a Filipino when they arrive in a foreign land. Many of us are very happy in Ireland because of its predominantly Catholic society. Despite the crises that have struck the Catholic Church in Ireland, Filipinos are edified by the deep faith they see in the lives of many Irish people.

Religion holds a central place in the life of most Filipinos. To them, religion is not an abstract belief system, but a collection of experiences, rituals and ceremonies that provide continuity in life, cohesion in the community and moral purpose for existence. Like the highly visible examples of flagellation and re-enacted crucifixion, processions and town fiestas in the Philippines, these movements may seem to have little in common with organised Christianity or Islam. But in the intensely personal religious context, they are extreme examples of how religion retains its central role in Philippine society.

Wherever they are in the world, Filipinos carry with them their religious practices. Catholic rituals are extremely different in Ireland, but soon after large groups of Filipinos settled here during the Celtic Tiger years, they found a way to organise simbang gabi at Christmas time. More and more Filipino organisations are coming up with fiestas for their patron saints back home. Couples for Christ are very active here, but the largest-scale activity so far is the annual novena to the Santo Niño. Based in St Joseph's Church on Berkeley Road in Dublin, the group organising the novena aims to continue the tradition and practices of Santo Niño devotion in Ireland and to propagate the devotion among other nationalities.

Filipino folk Christianity is also alive and well. You'll always find a Filipino priest at housewarmings and new business launches. Come what may, the Filipino Catholics will be the same wherever you find them.

A Church in Crisis

The scenario is different for Irish Christians. An editorial published in the *Irish Times* on 23 May 2016 noted that institutional Christianity in the country is in crisis. Congregations and the clergy are ageing, and there's a diminishing interest among the faithful, especially the working class, in attending liturgies. The main churches, it seems, are becoming the preserve of the middle class and the elderly.

Many church watchers believe that secularisation has led to the diminishing numbers of Irish Christians. Since the sexual revolution

204

that swept Western Europe and the U.S. in the 1960s, a growing number of Irish people have been questioning the authority of religious institutions. Whilst the percentage of Irish Christians remains high compared to the rest of Europe, problems are still rising.

Aside from secularisation, the clergy sex abuse scandals that rocked the Catholic Church in the 1990s was a major factor. The scandals made it unfashionable to declare oneself a practising Catholic; there was now social stigma in attending Mass, whereas decades ago, not going would have been a cause of embarrassment.

In spite of the decline in Church membership, however, a majority of the Irish still consider themselves to be Catholic. In the 2011 census, 84% stated that their religion was Roman Catholicism.

Some analysts contend that the Irish have learned to separate the concepts of 'religion' and 'faith' from each other. Whilst most Irish Catholics will balk at traditional religious practices that they feel are outdated, or socially and ethically backward, they haven't given up their faith. They go to church on special occasions, choose to get married in a church, and will want their funerals to be blessed by a priest.

Despite their nominal attendance at Sunday Masses, the Irish have retained the virtue of charity. This is why it's easy to raise thousands of euros for a good cause, even if the recipients are in some remote area in Asia or Africa.

I have seen many times this strong display of faith and generosity among the Irish. In 2006, typhoon Reming (international name Durian) hit the province of Albay in the Bicol region shortly after Mayon Volcano erupted. A total of 1,399 people were killed in the region that year. Casualties were caused by the flood intensified by lahar from the volcano.

When a group of Filipinos, including myself, sought help from the parish priest of St. Mary's Church in Lucan, a fundraising drive called 'Pancakes for the Philippines' was immediately launched. Within the first few hours of selling pancakes, we managed to collect €3,400! It was an unbelievable response.

On 8 November 2013, the super-typhoon Haiyan, known in the Philippines as Yolanda, left widespread devastation in its wake. Once again, thousands of euros were raised for the thousands of victims by different fundraising initiatives in various parts of Ireland.

The Pocket World in Figures 2014 named Ireland the world's top 'giver'. In a single month, 60 per cent of the population either donated money to charity, gave time to those in need or helped a stranger.

Christianity is alive and well in Ireland!

EPILOGUE

I'm home! By home I mean that I now have a better understanding of my culture and traditions, and have experienced enlightenment and acceptance of my Filipinohood. Home to self-awareness and recognising my own stereotypes and prejudices, and being open to attitudinal conversion.

Home is belonging in my adoptive country—this beautiful island which has been my sanctuary and haven for the last 38 years. Yes, I am who I am, a Filipino, a human being in Ireland, and a member of the great human race, understanding that we're all brothers and sisters wherever we come from, and whatever our culture and our religion.

Yet I belong to a unique race, no matter what. Filipinos are unique. And I have wondered several times how we, as Filipino migrant parents, can impart our values and cultural heritage to our children.

Can we, as first-generation Filipino migrants, make this a project for the second generation? For immigrant families like ours, one generation has to take the necessary step of ensuring that the next generation can have a sense of belonging.

Keeping our heritage alive: Filipinos in Ireland celebrating Independence Day

Perhaps we can learn from the second-generation Filipinos in the UK, who have been working on reconnecting to their roots through the years. Now that we have the European Network of Filipino Diaspora (EnFiD) here in Ireland, we have young, enthusiastic Filipinos to lead the way.

There's a beautiful video on YouTube, uploaded in 2009, that features members of Philippine Generations, a group of second-generation Filipinos working to awaken young UK-based Filipinos' interest in their parents' culture. One segment has a member of the

208

group, Alona, telling her daughter Anne the story of her mother's journey from the Philippines to the UK, along with her own journey of discovery:

Ang Kuwento ni Nanay ('My Mother's Story')

Once upon a time Lola travelled many miles in this land of hope. They worked hard but the masters did not always treat them right.

So when they had children, they were wary and did not teach them of their faraway sunshine.

As the children grew up, they were puzzled and did not know about their home.

The story ends with these lines:

They saw the other children enjoy their differentness.
And the children of the sunshine land thought, 'We must find out and not hide anymore.'

BIBLIOGRAPHY

Publications From and About the Philippines and Filipinos

Abella, Domingo. *Catalogo Alfabetico de Appelidos* (1849), National Archives Publication No.D-3, 1973.

Adeney, Miriam. 'Is There a Real Philippine Culture?'. *All Things to All Men: An Introduction to Missions in Filipino Culture,* edited by Evelyn Miranda-Feliciano, New Day, 1988.

Agoncillo, Teodoro. *A Short History of the Philippines.* Mentor Books, 1969.

Agoncillo, Teodoro, and Oscar Alfonso. *History of the Filipino People.* Malaya Books, 1968.

Aguilos, Stephen B. *Church Realities in the Philippines: 1900–1965.* Leyte-Samar Historical Society, 1999.

Alburo, Erlinda K. 'La Dulce Estranjera'. *SUMAD: Essays for the Centennial of the Revolution in Cebu.* De La Salle University Press, 1999.

Alejandro, Reynaldo G. *Fiesta! Fiesta!: Fiesta Festival Foods of the*

Philippines. KCC Innovations Inc., 2008.

Andres, Tomas. *Effective Discipline Through Filipino Values.* Rex Book Store, 1996.

Arguillas, Florio, Jr. 'The Transnational Families of Filipinos Nurses in the Midst of an Emerging Philippines-Ireland Migration System'. MA Thesis, Cornell University, 2009.

Austin, Craig. *The Lineage, Life and Labors of Jose Rizal, Philippine Patriot.* Philippine Education Company, 1913.

Bautista, Ma. Lourdes S., and Kingsley Bolton. *Philippine English: Linguistic and Literary Perspectives.* Hong Kong University Press, 2009.

Bulatao, Jaime SJ. *Split Level Christianity.* 3rd ed, Ateneo de Manila University Press, 1966.

Carroll, John J. *Philippine Institutions.* Solidaridad Publishing House, 1970.

Chaffee, Frederic H., and Nena Vreeland. *Area Handbook for the Philippines.* For sale by the Supt. of Docs., U.S. Govt. Print. Off., 1976.

Coates, Austin. *Rizal: Philippine Nationalist and Martyr.* Oxford University Press, 1968.

Collins, Neil. *The Splendid Cause: The Missionary Society of St. Columban 1916–1954.* The Columba Press, 2009.

Cordero-Fernado, Gilda. *Philippine Food and Life.* Anvil Publishing, 1992.

Corpuz, Onofre D. *The Philippines*. Prentice Hall, 1965.

Espinosa, Doray. 'English in the Philippines'. *Global Issues in Languages*. March 1997, no. 26, p.9.

Galang, Zoilo, and Camilo Osias, eds. *Encyclopedia of the Philippines*. Philippine Education Center, 1936.

Gowing, Peter G., and Robert D. McArnis, eds. *The Muslim Filipinos*. Solidaridad Publishing House, 1974.

Gorospe, Vitaliano R. *Filipino Values Revisited*. National Book Store, Inc., 1988.

Llangco, Mark Oliver S. 'Transnationalised Belonging: Second Generation Filipinos in England'. Dissertation, The University of Birmingham, 2013.

Guerrero, León Ma. *The First Filipino: A Biography of Jose Rizal*. National Heroes Commission, 1963.

Mercado, Leonardo N., ed. *Filipino Religious Psychology*. Divine Word University, 1977.

Newman, Yasmin. *7000 Islands: A Food Portrait of the Philippines*. Hardie Grant Books, 2014.

Nititham, Diane Sabenacio. 'The Personal is Global: Filipina Migrant Workers in the Irish Care Economy'. Irish Social Policy Association Postgraduate Conference, University College Dublin, Ireland, 20 July 2007.

O'Brien, Niall. *Revolution from the Heart*. Oxford University Press, 1997.

Ocampo, Ambeth R. *Rizal Without the Overcoat.* Anvil Publishing Inc, 1990.

Ofilada, Macario. *Errante Golondrina: The Life and Times of Josephine Bracken.* New Day Publishers, 2003.

Ramos, Maximo D. *Creatures of Philippine Lower Mythology.* University of the Philippines Press, 1971.

Roces, Alejandro R. *Fiesta.* Vera-Reyes, 1980.

Roley, Brian Ascalon. *American Son: A Novel.* W.W. Norton, 2010.

Taguinod, Fidel. 'Licensed to Care: Inhabiting the Transnational Economy of "Global Pinoy"'. Dissertation, Dublin Institute of Technology, 2013.

Publications From and About Ireland

Bluett, Anthony. *Things Irish.* Mercier Press, 1994.

Devoy, RJN. 'Sea Level Changes and Ireland'. *Technology Ireland,* vol. 22, no. 5, 1990, pp. 24–30.

Donovan, D, and AE Murphy. *The Fall of the Celtic Tiger: Ireland and the Euro Debt Crisis.* Oxford University Press, 2013.

Graham, Brian, ed. *In Search of Ireland: A Cultural Geography.* Routledge, 1997.

Griffin, Fiona. *Why Do the Irish?* The Linguaviva Centre, 1991.

Hegarty, Shane. *The Irish (and Other Foreigners): From the First People to the Poles.* Gill and MacMillan Ltd., 2009.

MacSharry, Ray, and Padraic White. *The Making of the Celtic Tiger: The Inside Story of Ireland's Boom Economy*. Mercier Press, 2000.

Murray, John. *Handbook for Travellers in Ireland*. 2nd ed, J Murray, 1866.

Murray, Marie. *When Times Are Tough*. Veritas Publications, 2011.

Wells, John SG, and C Niall McElwee. 'The recruitment crisis in nursing: placing Irish psychiatric nursing in context — a review'. *Journal of Advanced Nursing*, vol. 22, no.1, 2000, pp. 10–18.

Other Publications

Kluckholn, Clyde, and Henry Alexander Murray. *Personality in Nature, Society and Culture*. Knopf, 1953.

Oberg, Kalervo. 'Cultural Shock: Adjustment to New Cultural Environments'. *Missiology: An International Review*, vol. 7, no. 4, 1960.

Schneider, Susan, and Jean-Louis Barsoux. *Managing Across Cultures*. Pearson Education, 2002.

Takenaka, Masao. *God Is Rice: Asian Culture and Christian Faith*. Wipf and Stock Publishers, 2009.

Online Resources

Assad, Anna. 'Philippine Laws on Divorce, Separation and
    Annulment'. *LegalZoom*, http://info.legalzoom.com/philippine-
    laws-divorce-separation-annulment-20694.html. Accessed 7
    November 2016.

Canave-Dioquino, Corazon. 'Philippine Music: A Historical
    Overview'. *National Commission for Culture and the Arts*, 15 April
    2015, http://ncca.gov.ph/subcommissions/subcommission-on-
    the-arts-sca/music/philippine-music-a-historical-overview/.

Carbery, Genevieve. 'Migrants must "seduce" Irish, says sociologist'.
    The Irish Times, 5 September 2013,
    http://www.irishtimes.com/news/social-affairs/migrants-must-
    seduce-irish-says-sociologist-1.1516208. Accessed 5 November
    2016.

Estella, C. 'Lack of nurses burdens an ailing healthcare system'.
    Philippine Center for Investigative Journalism, 20 March 2005,
    http://www.pcij.org/stories/print/2005/nurses.html.

Fernquest, Jon. 'Filipino singers: Whole world is their stage'. *Bangkok
    Post*, 7 July 2012,
    http://www.bangkokpost.com/learning/advanced/301266/filip
    ino-singers-whole-world-is-their-stage.

Laranas, Gin de Mesa. 'Will the Philippines finally legalize divorce?'
    The New York Times, 28 July 2016,

https://www.nytimes.com/2016/07/29/opinion/will-the-philippines-finally-legalize-divorce.html?_r=0.

'Mercy Network: Philippines'. *Sisters of Mercy Worldwide.* http://www.mercyworld.org/mercy_network/index.cfm?loadref =86. Accessed 7 July 2015.

Medina, Isagani R. 'Wife of Dr. Jose Rizal' *Knights of the Order of Rizal,* http://knightsofrizal.org/?p=290. Accessed 19 June 2014.

Presentation Sisters. Union of the Sisters of the Presentation of the Blessed Virgin Mary, http://www.pbvm.org/. Accessed 11 May 2016.

Santos, Ana P. 'Ending a Marriage in the Only Country That Bans Divorce'. *The Atlantic,* 25 June 2015, https://www.theatlantic.com/international/archive/2015/06/di vorce-philippines-annulment/396449/. Accessed 20 April 2017.

'Story of Irish Music'. *Traditional Irish Musical Pub Crawl,* https://www.musicalpubcrawl.com/story-of-irish-music/. Accessed 20 November 2016.

'We Are. . .' *YouTube,* uploaded by Katrina Kirkwood, 4 August 2009, https://www.youtube.com/watch?v=_OBs5fyGVnU.

Wikipedia contributors. 'Folk music of Ireland.' *Wikipedia, The Free Encyclopedia,* 5 May 2017, https://en.wikipedia.org/wiki/Folk_music_of_Ireland. Accessed 7 May 2017.

APPENDIX

HISTORIC IRISH-FILIPINO CONNECTIONS

Our National Hero and His Irish Love

Jose Rizal and Josephine Bracken's relationship was not a smooth-sailing one. When the couple decided to get married after a month of courtship, Josephine's adoptive father, Mr Taufer, flew into a violent rage. Unable to endure the thought of losing Josephine, he tried to commit suicide by cutting his throat with a razor.

Rizal, however, grabbed Mr Taufer's wrists and stopped him from killing himself. To avoid further tragedy, Josephine returned to Manila with Mr Taufer by the first available steamer the next day.

217

After six months, Josephine returned to Dapitan. Doña Teodora, Jose's mother, permitted her son to marry Josephine, but Fr Antonio Obach of Dapitan refused to marry them without a special dispensation from the Bishop of Cebu.

Because Rizal was a Mason and Josephine was a Roman Catholic, they did not get a dispensation. The couple had no choice but to settle for a common-law marriage, with a ceremony witnessed by two people. They lived together as husband and wife in an octagonal bamboo house that Josephine turned into a love nest— stocking the pantry with pickles and preserves; cooking, washing, and finding food when supplies ran low; and trying desperately to build bridges with Jose's family, especially his sisters who were scandalized by rumours that Josephine was a woman of the streets and a tavern singer in Hong Kong.

In his letter to his younger sister Trinidad on 15 January 1896, Rizal wrote, 'we have no quarrels and we always laugh happily.' However, this love affair was no fairy tale. Bickering and arguments started after some time, one of which, according to an article in the *Philippines Free Press*, was violent enough to lead to Josephine having a miscarriage. The same article suggested that Rizal's request to be sent to Cuba as a medical volunteer was prompted by his dissatisfaction with his young partner.

On his way to Cuba, however, Rizal was arrested and, after a mock trial, sentenced to death by Spanish authorities. On 29 December 1896, Josephine visited Rizal in his cell. Rizal, upon seeing

218

here, sadly exclaimed: 'Ah! My dear, my time has come to be united with you but to be separated forever.' He then begged for forgiveness for the sorrows he had caused her.

Minutes before he calmly faced the firing squad, Rizal was finally given permission to marry Josephine. He gave her a copy of Fr Thomas á Kempis's *De La Imitacion de Cristo y Menosprecio del Mundo* with the dedication: 'To my dear and unhappy wife, Josephine, December 30th, 1896, Jose Rizal'. Josephine became a widow at just the age of 20.

Josephine asked the Spanish authorities for Rizal's remains, but they refused. She swore to avenge his death by joining Gen Emilio Aguinaldo's revolutionary movement on 6 January 1897. She once led a charge against the Spaniards and killed one Spanish officer, using her own rifle. She participated in many battles, and most of the time, she was hungry and barefooted.

Josephine witnessed the Tejeros Convention of the Magdalo and Magdiwang factions of the Katipunan at San Francisco de Malabon in Cavite. She was then summoned by Governor-General Camilo Polavieja who gave her an ultimatum to leave the country. Frightened by the threat of impending torture, she left Manila for Hong Kong in May 1897.

When her foster father died, Josephine married Don Vicente Abad of Cebu, who was then working in a tabacalera in Hong Kong, on 15 December1898. They had one daughter, Dolores Abad, who

219

was born on 27 April 1900 in Hong Kong, and who eventually married Don Salvador Mina of Ilocos Sur. When Dolores was one year old, her parents brought her to the Philippines, and they lived with the other Abads in a big house in Calle Magdalena, Tondo, Manila.

According to the American historian Craig Austin, Josephine also lived for some time in Cebu where she taught English, first as a private tutor, and later on as a public schoolteacher. It is said that one of her students was Sergio Osmeña, who later became the second President of the Commonwealth of the Philippines.

Afflicted by tuberculosis of the larynx, Josephine wished to die in Hong Kong. A certain Father Spada, then Vicar General of Hong Kong, said that he was deeply touched upon seeing her deplorable condition. She was broken down in health and in spirit, and had lost all her hope and faith in humanity.

Father Spada took Josephine to the Saint Francis Hospital where nuns took good care of her. On the eve of her death, she asked for the Holy Sacrament, which Father Spada and another priest administered. She died on 15 March 1902, unaware that a line of her husband's poem had rendered her immortal: *'Adiós, dulce estranjera, mi amiga, mi alegría.'* ('Farewell, sweet foreigner, my darling, my delight.')

She was buried in the Catholic section of the Happy Valley Cemetery in Hong Kong.

Fr Kevin McHugh and Fr Martin Murphy, Columban

missionary priests who worked for many years in the Philippines, helped unearth Josephine's Irish roots. Both priests were admirers of Rizal and wanted to help prove that Josephine was an Irishwoman.

Fr McHugh traced the military postings of James Bracken, Josephine's father. He found out that Josephine was indeed born in Hong Kong to Irish couple Corporal James and Elizabeth Bracken, and was the youngest of four children. The three other children were born in Ireland, Malta and Gibraltar. On his retirement from military service, James Bracken settled and died in Dublin, although he originally came from Ferbane, Co. Offaly.

Fr Martin Murphy was responsible for tracing the Dublin descendants of Josephine Bracken. Using the Irish telephone directory, he sent letters to a selected number of James Brackens. His efforts were rewarded when one day in 1997, he received a call from Francis Bracken in Dublin, who confirmed that his great-great-grandfather James was Josephine's father. Fr Murphy happily filled him in on the love story of his grand-aunt Josephine and her first husband, the Philippines' national hero and martyr.

Irish Missionaries in the Philippines

'The Philippines—a sort of Catholic Ireland off the coastline of Asia.'

The RTE documentary *On God's Mission*, televised in March

2009, drove home to me the significance and remarkable contribution of Irish missionaries to the Philippines. The documentary recorded 'the incredible story of how some of Ireland's best and brightest individuals left Ireland far behind them, and brought their skills, energy and entrepreneurial flair to those less fortunate in many parts of the world.' We Filipinos were among the recipients of those gifts.

As a former member of one of 12 parishes run by the Columban Fathers in Zambales, I saw for myself the selfless intentions of the Irish missionaries to Christianise the locals. Yes, the Spanish friars brought us Christianity but with the ulterior motive of subjugating us for the benefit of the empire. The Irish, however, arrived to 'colonise' for God, not for an empire.

'For a missionary society, the home country is not a base from which an army goes forth,' an article in the Columban *Far East* magazine's 50th anniversary issue states. "It is rather a great Christian family, living by a generous love that also drives men to go out and share it with other men. It is a spiritual powerhouse that comforts and supports them there, drawing God's grace on their work.'

Thousands of Filipinos were educated and spiritually nourished by the Irish. In Zambales, the Columban Fathers built not only churches but a school in every parish. The Redemptorists pioneered parishes in many a remote town in the Visayas.

The De La Salle Brothers established university education in

Manila, and the Blessed Sacrament Fathers provided prayer centres in urban places. There are the Divine Word Fathers (SVDs) in Ilocos and Dumaguete, who pioneered education for the poor, the Sisters of Mercy in the Visayas with their health programmes, the Presentation Sisters in Mindanao with their pastoral care schemes, and several other congregations who are still engaged in many educational, spiritual and pastoral services throughout the islands.

More recently, we remember Fr. Michael Sinnot who was kidnapped and eventually released by a gang in Mindanao. Minister Michael Martin, then Irish Secretary of Foreign Affairs, remarked on his release:

> 'Fr. Michael Sinnott, a member of the Columban Fathers, displayed great forbearance in enduring more than a month in captivity, in spite of his age and difficult health. Fr. Michael has spent much of his life working for the poorest of the poor in the Philippines...'

I don't know of any Filipino who's not aware of the Wednesday devotion in Baclaran, but few probably know that it's a legacy of the Irish Redemptorist Fathers. Every Wednesday, an estimated 100,000 faithful come to the Redemptorist Church in Baclaran, Metro Manila to pray the Novena to our Lady of Perpetual Help. On the first Wednesday of the month, that number expands to 120,000.

Who is the Catholic Filipino who has not visited in faith and devotion the Blessed Sacrament Church, run by Irish SSS Fathers, in Sta. Cruz, Manila? The Congregation of the Blessed Sacrament was founded in Paris, France in 1856 by Father Eymard. All his life, he

223

searched for an answer to the deep spiritual hungers of his day, and he discovered it in the Eucharist. Inspired by this sacrament, he inaugurated a new way of life in the Church, one completely shaped by the Eucharist celebrated, contemplated and lived in communion.

By prayer before the Blessed Sacrament and an active apostolic life, the Irish priests strive to make Christ in the Eucharist better known and loved. They live together and work together to show the fruits of the Eucharist.

The legacy of Irish missionaries is, however, not limited to prayers and devotions, administering sacraments, and building churches and schools. In response to the changes in the Church following Vatican II in the 1960s and several crises in Philippine society, the Irish mission started to expand the scope and nature of their apostolic work.

Building basic ecclesial communities became the pastoral thrust of mission programmes. The laity as people of God were recognised, and their participation in the running of catechetical programmes, and justice and peace groups became essential. Lay formation institutes were set up, and retreat houses and formation programmes were established throughout the country.

The use of mass media as a means of evangelisation was deemed necessary, hence, radio stations and other media facilities were arranged, with a number of confreres involved in social action and television programming.

The declaration of Martial Law in 1972 and the Marcos dictatorship brought new challenges to the Church and missionaries. Missionaries adopted the message of justice and liberation and, together with the local clergy and lay leaders, preached explicitly the liberating message of the Gospel by denouncing injustices.

In his book *Revolution from the Heart*, Fr Niall O'Brien explained how, by imprisoning him, the Marcos regime tried to silence him and many others within the Church who were increasingly speaking out against social and political injustice. The move backfired against the government when his imprisonment became the subject of international protest and a focus of the escalating Philippine movement for non-violent change. The O'Brien event became a precursor for many other members of the clergy to take their stand and prove that the true meaning of Christian discipleship is unconditional commitment to the poor and the oppressed.

The election of Corazon Aquino as President and the subsequent peaceful People Power revolution that followed Marcos's refusal to respect the people's decision ended 14 years of dictatorship in the Philippines and started the journey back to democracy.

During the Marcos years, hundreds of Irish missionaries worked in the Philippines. Today there are only about 90 Irish missionaries left, working mostly in poor communities. Several nuns and priests have died, majority have grown old and ill and are now spending their remaining days in Irish nursing homes.

'If you're a good missionary,' declared Sister Cait Coyle in a recent RTE television series, 'you'll start work and then hand it over to the locals. The country and the church are in their hands now. They have their own bishops, priests and nuns. We're not needed anymore.'

Thanks in a big way to the generosity of Irish and many other foreign missionaries, the Philippines today is not only the largest Christian nation in Asia but also the third largest Catholic nation in the world. It is home to many of the world's major religious congregations—the Augustinians, Dominicans, Jesuits and Redemptorists. These religious establishments are now successfully being run by Filipino bishops, priests and nuns.

We Came, We Saw, We Stayed: The Celtic Tiger Era (1998–2008)

There were less than 300 Filipinos in Ireland in the 1970s and 1980s. We lived in total obscurity, coming into focus only when news on a natural disaster, extreme poverty or Martial Law injustices hit the headlines.

We now have around 13,000 Filipinos currently living in Ireland, working in various sectors of the economy. However, nursing is still the most dominant Filipino occupation in Ireland.

James Reilly, recently appointed Minister for Health, declared:

'The Filipino nurses as health professionals, have been a very welcome addition to our health services. Their excellent education and training system provided nurses of very high caliber to work in Ireland.'

Our Lady's Hospital in Crumlin, the largest children's hospital in Ireland, cares for over 120,000 children annually. The hospital was one of the places to benefit from the arrival of Filipino nurses to make up for a shortage of Irish nurses. Lorcan Birthistle, Chief Executive, says:

'Clinical competence, a good heart, a helping hand and a pleasant personality is what makes Filipino nurses stand out. The children and families of Ireland are indebted to them for their commitment to children's nursing.'

Nurses from the Philippines commenced employment in Connolly Hospital in 2001. Over the next six years, significant numbers of Filipinos continued to arrive, and there are now 129 Filipino nurses on staff.

'Their contribution to Connolly Hospital,' testifies Mary Walshe, Hospital Manager, 'has been immense in that they have enabled the Nursing Service to have appropriate staffing levels to maintain a quality service. A number of staff have been promoted and are excelling in their management role. They have enriched the culture of the hospital and the hospital is proud to have such valuable committed members of staff.'

Meanwhile, at Cork University Hospital, Mary Mills, Director of Nursing, has this to say:

'It has been a decade since we recruited nurses from the Philippines to work with us. As the only level 1 trauma centre in Ireland, we are recognized for our high standards of excellence and care. Our Filipino colleagues integrated well into our hospital and their personal and professional nursing experience has continued to deliver a caring service to our patients over the years.'

The Filipino nurses' strategic importance in the health care system sparked policy changes to address their concerns and prevent them from leaving, which eventually benefitted other immigrants in Ireland. This is illustrated by the Family Reunification Programme, which enabled the nurses' spouses and children to join them here. Initially, spouses were not automatically allowed to work in the country, but the Filipino League of Nurses, through several Irish NGOs, worked to have this rule changed. Now, qualified spouses of immigrant workers are permitted to work.

ABOUT THE AUTHOR

Vising Benavidez-Kennedy has been living in Ireland for the last 38 years. She is co-founder of the first Filipino-Irish Association in Ireland (1980) which she chaired five times in its lifetime of twenty years.

Vising is a journalism graduate from the University of Santo Tomas in Manila, Philippines. She worked with *The Manila Chronicle* for three years, first as a provincial correspondent and staff member of the provincial section, before being appointed staff writer for the publication's *Saturday Weekly Magazine* in 1967.

Sadly, the newspaper was shut down by the government shortly after President Marcos declared Martial Law. Vising went to edit *The Echo*, the house organ of the Sisters of St. Paul of Chartres, Philippines. Arriving in Ireland in 1977 with her husband Jim, she became a contributing feature writer for the *Woman's Way* magazine, a Smurfit publication in Dublin.

At the height of the Celtic Tiger years, she edited *The Filipino Forum* (2004–2012) and wrote a column for *Metro Eireann* (2006–2010), the only multicultural newspaper in Ireland. She was an active volunteer at St. Mary's Church in the parish of Lucan, serving as a member of the Parish Pastoral Council, the Bereavement group, Minister of the Word, Baptismal Group, and Justice and Peace group. She also co-founded the Lucan Gardening Club. Now retired, she lives with her husband Jim in Lucan, Co. Dublin. They have two grown-up children, Patrick and Noriana.

71288068R00127

Made in the USA
Columbia, SC
28 May 2017